IMPACT ASSESSMENT IN THE EU

THE STATE OF THE ART
AND THE ART OF THE STATE

ANDREA RENDA

CENTRE FOR EUROPEAN POLICY STUDIES
BRUSSELS

The Centre for European Policy Studies (CEPS) is an independent policy research institute based in Brussels. Its mission is to produce sound analytical research leading to constructive solutions to the challenges facing Europe today.

The views expressed in this report are those of the author writing in a personal capacity and do not necessarily reflect those of CEPS or any other institution with which he is associated.

Andrea Renda is a Senior Research Fellow at CEPS, where he is head of the Regulatory Affairs Programme.

ISBN 92-9079-600-6

Centre for European Policy Studies
Place du Congrès 1, B-1000 Brussels
Tel: 32 (0) 2 229.39.11 Fax: 32 (0) 2 219.41.51
e-mail: info@ceps.be
Website: http://www.ceps.be

TABLE OF CONTENTS

List of Figures

List of Boxes

FOREWORD

Like computer systems and like all human beings, policy-makers always use proxies. Examples are countless. On the one hand, competition authorities take consumer welfare as a proxy for social welfare, perfect competition as a proxy for the maximisation of consumer welfare, market shares as a proxy for market power and evidence of price parallelism as a proxy for collusion. And sometimes they are wrong. On the other hand, regulators, striving to mimic the functioning of perfectly competitive markets, infer from market failures the need to abandon *laissez-faire* principles and to regulate, using proxies to assess the impact of future and existing regulations. Increasingly, they are required to assess the past, present and future direct and indirect costs and benefits of regulations, and to justify intervention on the basis of such estimations. In so doing, they sometimes err.

When it comes to regulatory impact assessment, the scientific ambition of economics is heavily challenged: a crystal ball enabling a full vision of the future social, environmental and economic impact of proposed regulations is nowhere to be found. After all, this brings bad news and good news. The bad news is that *ex ante* impact assessment is no panacea, and is doomed to be always found imperfect and – to a certain extent – arbitrary. The good news is that, notwithstanding such imperfection, well-crafted methods of impact assessment can instil a greater degree of 'awareness', transparency, efficiency and accountability in the policy process. As a matter of fact, scholars in many fields of the social sciences have discovered that regulatory impact assessment and cost-benefit analysis can provide the best contribution to the quality of legislation when those in charge of implementing them are aware of both their potential and their inherent limit. The Socratic motto 'γνωθι σεαυτον', here, is to be kept on the desk, always. This is, indeed, the difficult 'Art of the State'.

In this monograph, I focus on the latest EU experience in developing methods for *ex ante* assessment of the economic, social and environmental impacts of major proposed regulations. My work aims at stimulating discussion amongst scholars and policy-makers on the upcoming review of the EU integrated impact assessment model, scheduled for early 2006. I offer it, however, with a caveat: like computers, policy-makers and all other human beings, I also used a number of proxies throughout the work – in choosing scorecard items, relying on previous streams of literature, formulating roadmaps and, more generally, in my attempt to provide a static picture of an inherently dynamic process. Hence, I also may be wrong, and apologise if some readers find my conclusions insufficiently firm.

I have been thinking about a monograph on impact assessment for quite a long time. The idea did not materialise, however, until Daniel Gros and Karel Lannoo offered me the opportunity to start and manage the Regulatory Affairs Programme at the Centre for European Policy Studies, in Brussels. From such a privileged position, I have had the chance to fully appraise the features and paradoxes of EU better regulation, and apply my previous theoretical studies to the field observation of impact assessment practices in the EU, the US and the UK. For this reason, my first acknowledgment goes to Daniel and Karel for giving me this opportunity. I also would like to thank Jacques Pelkmans for his valuable comments and suggestions, Davide Cortesini for drawing an outstanding Möbius strip, which adorns the cover, and Anne Harrington and Els Van den Broeck for patient and creative editorial advice. Needless to say, some useful hints in this monograph are not mine, unlike all errors and imperfections.

Andrea Renda
Senior Research Fellow, CEPS

EXECUTIVE SUMMARY

In the frantic environment surrounding the European Union after the French and Dutch 'no' votes on the Constitutional Treaty, EU policy-makers are striving to identify the key drivers that will lead Europe back on track. 'Competitiveness' is the keyword in Brussels now, and one of the recognised drivers of competitiveness is 'better regulation'. As a matter of fact, the EU Better Regulation Action Plan is perceived as one of the most crucial milestones for achieving the ambitious Lisbon Goals.[1] The European Commission itself recently acknowledged that Europe's "disappointing economic performance" calls for further action in the field of better regulation, in order to stimulate growth and employment by streamlining the regulatory environment, with stronger emphasis on the principles of proportionality and subsidiarity in developing more cost-effective regulatory tools, and enhanced focus on cutting red tape.[2]

Recently, efforts to improve the quality of EU regulation have relied on the full implementation of the new EU Integrated Impact Assessment (IIA) model introduced in 2002,[3] in the wake of the Mandelkern Report.[4]

---

[1] The European Commission Action Plan on simplifying and improving the regulatory environment (COM(2002) 278) was part of a wider better regulation package launched in June 2002.

[2] See the European Commission Communication, "Better regulation for growth and jobs in the European Union", COM(2005)97, 16 March 2005. In the press release, the Commission introduced the equation of "Less red tape = more growth" (see Press Release, IP/05/311, 16 March 2005). For a description of the Commission's new approach, see section 2.3.

[3] The IIA model was introduced on 5 June 2002, with a European Commission Communication on impact assessment (COM(2002) 276), which included guidelines on how to carry out an extended impact assessment, entitled "Impact

The 2003 Interinstitutional Agreement on Better Regulation, the joint Letter of the Irish and three incoming presidents of ECOFIN filed on January 2004, the 'Doorn motion' within the Legal Affairs Committee of the European Parliament and the joint statement issued on December 2004 by the Irish, Dutch, Luxembourg, UK, Austrian and Finnish Presidencies on "Advancing Regulatory Reform" are all evidence of a growing interest in linking impact assessment to competitiveness at the EU level.[5] The Commission itself reacted by launching a new strategy for the simplification of the regulatory environment and by issuing a new Communication on Better Regulation in March 2005, as well as new Guidelines on Impact Assessment three months later. More recently, Commission Vice-President Günther Verheugen stated that in the coming years all EU regulatory initiatives will have to pass muster under the IIA model, announcing that the Commission "will only put forward proposals that have undergone an impact assessment" and that "this approach should guarantee that we know the full costs and benefits of future legislation".[6]

So far, so good. But can Europe really live up to the promise? Does the EU impact assessment model truly possess the salvific virtues ascribed to it by EU policy-makers? Piercing the veil, available evidence reveals that the way in which the procedure has been implemented to date has resulted in a sea of disappointment. The quality of extended impact assessments appears to be low and is even decreasing over time. Commission DGs in charge of performing the assessment seem quite far from enabling greater awareness of "the full costs and benefits of future legislation". As will be explained in more detail below, of the 70 extended impact assessments completed before July 2005, only a few quantified or monetised the expected costs and benefits arising from the proposal. Only in a limited number of cases were business compliance costs assessed, and the same

---

Assessment in the Commission - Guidelines" and "A Handbook for Impact Assessment in the Commission - How to do an Impact Assessment", recently replaced by new "Impact Assessment Guidelines", SEC(2005)791, 15 June 2005.

[4] Mandelkern Group, Final Report, 2001 (available at *http://europa.eu.int/comm/secretariat_general/impact/docs/mandelkern.pdf*).

[5] All these recent initiatives are described in more detail below, in section 2.2.

[6] See Verheugen's speech at the UK Presidency Conference on Better Regulation, Edinburgh, 23 September 2005 (available at *http://www.cabinetoffice.gov.uk/regulation/documents/better_regulation_conference_speeches/pdf/050923_verheugen.pdf* – last visited 5 December 2005).

applies to administration costs. And when it comes to justifying the viability of a proposed new piece of legislation, things get even worse. As a matter of fact, the *cahier de doléances* is long enough to leave few beacons of hope: the gap between the *sein* and the *sollen* of EU impact assessment is, in one word, huge.

Against this worrying backdrop, the UK Presidency, which ran from July to December 2005 (a period coinciding with the completion of this monograph), has taken a significant departure in its approach to impact assessment from previous EU policy. But this should come as no surprise. Past evidence reveals that many of the most important steps towards the introduction and refinement of impact assessment procedures at EU level have occurred under UK Presidencies, and have heavily borrowed from the UK experience, undoubtedly the *avant-garde* of impact assessment at member state level.[7] The ambitious integrated impact assessment model adopted in 2003 is currently being replaced by a new approach, which mostly focuses on the need to 'cut red tape'.[8] In doing this, the UK Presidency is drawing heavily on its national 'better regulation' strategy, which led to drastic changes and, most recently, to a consultation for the enactment of a revolutionary Better Regulation Bill, as well as a cross-government initiative to measure and then cut administrative costs.[9]

In particular, the UK Presidency has put strong emphasis on the simplification of the existing regulatory environment and the reduction of administrative burdens. Following the so-called 'Hampton Review' in March 2005, the UK Government established a new Better Regulation Executive with the specific purpose of identifying areas for reducing regulatory burdens, under the motto 'less is more' which directly recalls the goal of achieving 'more value with less money' that lied at the core of the whole 'New Public Management' revolution in the UK in the early

---

[7] See section 1.3.

[8] See *Advancing Better Regulation in Europe*, discussion paper prepared by the UK, Austrian and Finnish Presidencies for consideration at the (ECOFIN) Council on 6 December, available at *http://register.consilium.eu.int/pdf/en/05/st15/st15140.en05.pdf* (visited on December 30, 2005).

[9] A description of the new UK initiative on better regulation is contained in section 1.2.2. See also the Better Regulation Executive's website (http://www.cabinetoffice.gov.uk/regulation/index.asp – last visited 5 December 2005).

1980s.[10] The UK Presidency has attempted to replicate such an initiative at the EU level, by focusing on the creation of a common methodology for assessing administrative burdens, based on the Standard Cost Model successfully implemented in the Netherlands, and on the promotion of the risk-based approach adopted after the UK 'Hampton Review'.

What remains to be seen and discussed, however, is whether this new approach will ultimately lead EU policy-makers to succeed in disentangling the conundrum of procedures and overlapping pieces of legislation that characterise most sectors of the EU economy, or whether further refinements will be needed in order to help EU and national administrations in the successful implementation of *ex ante* and *ex post* assessment. If anything, the changing landscape of impact assessment in the EU will require yet another effort for EU officials in charge of impact assessment. If a wholly new model is put in place, DGs in charge of impact assessment will have to become familiar with a new procedure, and this will slow down the process further – like in the myth of Sisyphus, condemned to an eternity of rolling a boulder uphill, to watch it roll back down again.

As the Commission has scheduled a comprehensive review of its impact assessment model for early 2006, the time has come to take stock of the results achieved so far in assessing the impact of legislation, and to look forward to the changes and refinements that would help the Commission to live up to the promise of setting up an efficient, transparent, effective and accountable impact assessment system. The ambition of this paper is to contribute to the identification of the steps to be followed in order to get the best out of impact assessment and better regulation at EU and member state level.

Chapter 1 briefly describes the state of the art in impact assessment, contrasting some of the most successful models implemented at national level – most notably, the US and UK experiences – and the EU Integrated Impact Assessment model. Chapter 2 contains a scorecard analysis of the 70

---

[10] The 'new public management' revolution in the UK was inspired by a stream of literature that advocated a more performance-oriented culture amongst public bureaucrats and a wider use of outsourcing, market-type mechanisms and public-private partnerships for the delivery of public services. See Jan Erik Lane, *New Public Management,* London: Routledge, 2000; and most notably Christopher Pollitt and Geert Bouckaert, *Public Management Reform. A Comparative Analysis*, Oxford: Oxford University Press, 2000.

extended impact assessments performed by Commission DGs until July 2005, discussing the results of the analysis and describing the actions that have been undertaken by the Commission, the Council and the Parliament in order to strengthen the use of such a regulatory tool. Chapter 3 proposes a number of 'roadmaps' for improving the efficiency and effectiveness of the EU model in the years to come, with a view to getting (at least close) to the Lisbon goals by 2010. Chapter 4 offers conclusions.

1. Impact Assessment Models

The use of impact assessment tools has become widespread in OECD countries over the past two decades. Countries that successfully introduced a culture of impact assessment in their regulatory processes include, most notably, the US, UK, Canada, Australia and New Zealand – all of which share, not surprisingly, common law legal systems.[11] The first, complete procedure for assessing the costs and benefits of a proposed regulation was introduced in 1981 in the US, under the administration of President Ronald Reagan, although other attempts had been made in previous years with the 'Quality of Life Review' and the 'Inflation Impact Assessment' performed by the Council on Wage and Price Stability (CWPS).[12] The US model of impact assessment is nowadays so pervasive in US administrations that every year the US Office of Management and Budget (OMB) publishes a comprehensive calculation of the costs and benefits of regulations enacted over the previous year, the so-called "Yearly Report on the Costs and Benefits of Federal Regulations".[13] And, although a fierce debate has emerged both on the quality of government calculation of costs and benefits and on the soundness of the methodology adopted in performing

---

[11] See e.g. OECD, *Regulatory Impact Analysis: Best Practice in OECD Countries*, Paris, 1997; and more recently, *Regulatory Impact Analysis (RIA) Inventory*, Note by the Secretariat, 29th Session of the OECD Public Governance Committee, 15-16 April 2004, International Energy Agency, Paris.

[12] The 'Quality of Life Review' was introduced under the Nixon Administration with an OMB memorandum on "Agency regulations, standards, and guidelines pertaining to environmental quality, consumer protection, and occupational and public health and safety", 5 October 1971 (available at *http://www.thecre.com/ombpapers/QualityofLife1.htm* – last visited 5 December 2005). Subsequently, the Inflation Impact Assessment procedure was officially launched by Gerald Ford on 27 November 1974, with Executive Order 11,821 (available at *http://www.thecre.com/ombpapers/ExecutiveOrder11821.htm* – last visited 5 December 2005).

[13] See the OMB draft Report on the Costs and Benefits of Federal Regulations (available at *http://www.whitehouse.gov/omb/inforeg/regpol-reports_congress.html* – visited 5 December 2005).

ex ante assessments, the US experience is still to be considered the 'polar star' for EU policy-makers.[14]

Attempts to provide a comprehensive review of the EU economy have recently proliferated, especially after 2003 when the European Commission started developing a list of structural indicators of member states' progress towards the Lisbon goals.[15] More recently, the Commission has attempted to detect more specific links between ongoing sectoral reforms and overall progress, particularly in its 2005 report on the 'cost of non-Lisbon'.[16] However, a lot still needs to be done in devising new tools for *ex post* monitoring of the costs of EU regulations. Accordingly, it is worth taking stock by providing a brief description of some of the most relevant and insightful international experiences in *ex ante* and *ex post* assessment of the impact of regulations, most notably in the US and UK, before looking forward to next developments at Community level.

1.1 The US impact assessment model: The polar star

The United States was the first country to adopt a model of regulatory impact assessment. The earliest evidence of rules requiring the calculation of prospective costs and benefits of new regulations dates back to the Nixon administration, when US firms started complaining about the costs of regulation and uncontrolled 'regulatory creep', mostly as a result of newly passed environmental legislation.[17] The administration reacted with the so-called 'Quality of Life Review', which mandated a preliminary calculation of firms' costs resulting from compliance with new environmental rules as a fundamental pre-condition of good-quality

---

[14] See Box 2 in chapter 3, for a description of the current debate on the merits and soundness of current quantitative estimates provided by US federal agencies and, more generally, of quantitative benefit-cost analysis.

[15] The 2003 and 2004 reviews of the EU economy are available at *http://europa.eu.int/comm/economy_finance/publications/the_eu_economy_review_en.htm* – last visited 5 December 2005.

[16] See European Commission Staff Working Paper, *The Economic Costs of Non-Lisbon*, SEC(2005)385, 15 March 2005.

[17] For a short illustration of the major waves of regulatory reform in the US, see "The Role of Economic Analysis in Regulatory Reform", chapter 1 of OMB Report to Congress on the Costs and Benefits of Federal Regulations (available at *http://www.whitehouse.gov/omb/inforeg/chap1.html* – visited 5 December 2005).

regulation.[18] The Review, conceived as a privileged channel for public consultation, soon ended up enhancing the risk of regulatory capture, leaving legislative initiatives in the environmental field prey to aggressive and well-organised interest groups.[19]

Under the Ford administration, the US government showed an increased interest in promoting the use of cost-benefit analysis in assessing the prospective impact of proposed regulations. Executive Order 11,821, issued in 1974, mandated an Inflation Impact Assessment by federal agencies. Such procedure introduced an *ex ante* assessment of the expected impact of new regulatory measures on the inflation rate.[20] The creation of the Council on Wage and Price Stability aimed at ensuring that proposed regulations that were likely to exert a significant upward impact on nominal prices could be rejected in case they carried an incomplete or insufficient assessment of the inflationary impact.[21]

The Inflation Impact Assessment procedure can indeed be considered as a first version of what would later become the US Regulatory Impact Assessment (RIA) model. As a matter of fact, economists in the Council on Wage and Price Stability gradually transformed the mere estimation of the inflationary impact into a real cost-benefit analysis, to be used as a 'counter-argument' during public consultation processes mandated by the 1946 Administrative Procedure Act.[22] US President Gerald Ford amended

---

[18] "Quality of Life Review", op. cit.

[19] See L. Rodriguez, "Constitutional and Statutory Limits for Cost-Benefit Analysis Pursuant to Executive Orders 12291 and 12498", *Boston College Environmental Affair Law Review* 505, 512, 1988. See also, for a short description, Robert W. Hahn and Robert E. Litan, "Counting Regulatory Costs and Benefits: Lessons for the US and Europe", *Journal of International Economic Law*, Vol. 8, No. 2, 2005, p. 474.

[20] See e.g. M. Weidenbaum, *Regulatory Process Reform from Ford to Clinton*, CATO Institute, 2000 (available at *www.cato.org/pubs/regulation/reg20n1a.html* – visited 5 December 2005).

[21] See J. Morrall III, "Ebbs and Flows in the Quality of Regulatory Analysis", speech at the Weidenbaum Center Forum on Executive Regulatory Analysis: Surveying the Record, Making It Work, National Press Club, Washington, D.C., 17 December 2001 (available at *http://wc.wustl.edu/ExecutiveRegulatoryReviewTranscripts/Morrall.pdf* – visited 5 December 2005).

[22] See J. Morrall III, "An Assessment of the U.S. Regulatory Impact Assessment Program", in *Regulatory Impact Analysis: Best Practices in the Main OECD Countries*, OECD, Paris, 1997.

the inflation Impact Assessment model by issuing EO 11,949, and stating that "[t]he title of Executive Order No. 11,821 of November 27, 1974 is amended to read 'Economic Impact Statements'".[23]

A few years later, during the Carter administration, the 10 most relevant new regulations in each year's US government agenda were made the subject of extended *ex ante* assessment by a specialised ad hoc group of economists called the 'Regulatory Analysis Review Group'.[24] But the introduction of a more comprehensive regulatory impact assessment procedure only occurred under the Reagan administration.

1.1.1 The Reagan and Bush (Sr.) Administrations

Under the Reagan administration, with EO 12,291, issued in 1981, federal agencies were obliged to adopt a real regulatory impact analysis.[25] The Executive Office mandated a thorough reassessment of the existing regulation in force, for the purpose of identifying norms to be abolished or simplified. The evaluation and oversight of agencies' behaviour, previously performed by the CWPS, was taken on by OIRA (Office of Information and Regulatory Affairs), which was created within the Office of Management and Budget for the purpose of implementing the *1980 Paperwork Reduction Act*. OIRA was given the power to suspend regulations by sending them back to the sponsoring agency until a satisfactory cost-benefit analysis was performed. The OMB, as a result, became a sort of regulatory clearinghouse.

Since then, more than 1,000 proposed regulations have been scrutinised by the OMB. Possible contrasts between OMB and agencies were addressed with the help of a new Task Force on Regulatory Relief, chaired by then Vice-President George Bush, Sr.[26] The Task Force was also

---

[23] See Executive Order No. 11,949 of 31 December 1976 (available at *http://www.thecre.com/ombpapers/ExecutiveOrder11949.htm* – visited 5 December 2005).

[24] See Weidenbaum, op. cit.

[25] The text of EO 12,291 is available at *http://www.thecre.com/pdf/EO12291.PDF* (last visited 5 December 2005).

[26] The other members were the Secretary of the Treasury, Attorney General, Secretary of Commerce, Secretary of Labor, Director of OMB, Assistant to the President for Policy Development and the Chairman of the Counsel of Economic Advisers. See the White House's Fact Sheet on Reagan's Initiatives to Reduce Regulatory Burdens, 18 February 1981 (available at *http://www.thecre.com/*

asked to estimate the savings that could follow from a full implementation of the new RIA procedure. The result was striking: according to the administration, the new procedure produced yearly cost savings as high as $10-20 billion. This calculation was heavily criticised, however.[27] Similarly, the activity of the Task Force was subject to fierce opposition. The Reagan administration was accused of having drastically reduced the budget and personnel of federal agencies, achieving substantial decreases in the cost of regulation, but also a dramatic reduction in the number of proposals issued by federal agencies. As a consequence, in 1983, the Task Force was abolished and the OMB was given back its dominant role in the US RIA procedure.[28]

A second Executive Order, in 1985, required agencies to provide the OMB with detailed information on their regulatory agenda at the end of each year. This eventually paved the way for what has been termed the 'grand experiment', i.e. the OMB *Report to Congress on the Costs and Benefits of Federal Regulations*, a yearly publication that constitutes a unique example of a comprehensive, yearly calculation of total costs and benefits of the *corpus* of existing regulations.[29]

Under the Bush Sr. administration, the role formerly played by the Task Force on Regulatory Relief was assigned to the Council on Competitiveness, chaired by Vice-President Richard Quayle, which was given a mandate to abrogate all federal rules that could hinder the

---

pdf/Reagan_RegainInitiatives.pdf – last visited 5 December 2005). President Reagan identified regulatory relief as one of the four key elements for the recovery of the US economy. The results were nevertheless quite disappointing. See Reagan's Memorandum on the "Comprehensive Review of Federal Regulatory Programs", 15 December 1986; and the commentary by William A. Niskanen, "The Weak Fourth Leg of Reaganomics", *The Wall Street Journal* on 30 June 1988.

[27] See Weidenbaum, op. cit., and S. Breyer, "Regulation and Deregulation in the United States", in G. Majone (ed.), *De-regulation or Re-regulation? Regulatory Reform in Europe and the United States*, London: Pinter Publishers, 1990.

[28] See A. Morrison, "OMB Interference with Agency Rulemaking: The Wrong Way to Write a Regulation", *Harvard Law Review*, Vol. 99, No. 1059, 1986, p. 1062 (describing Reagan's EO as implicitly designed to ensure that regulation was only a 'last resort' option).

[29] See the description provided by Robert W. Hahn and Mary Beth Muething, "The Grand Experiment in Regulatory Reporting", *Administrative Law Review*, Vol. 55, No. 3, Summer, 2003, pp. 607-642.

competitiveness of US firms.[30] The main goal was to minimise regulatory burdens faced by the economy. Such a revolutionary attempt was strongly criticised by the Democrats and a number of economists, but also by federal agencies, Congressional Commissions and environmentalist associations, which lamented that the OMB (and in particular, the OIRA) exercised an excessive and unchallenged *veto* power on proposed regulations. Some commentators complained that OIRA and the White House had been captured by powerful interest groups, which inspired their intervention to stifle and repeal needed regulations, thus decreasing the transparency and accountability of federal rule-making. Institutional tension reached a peak when Congress refused to confirm a politically appointed agency director.[31]

According to an authoritative commentator, the excessive centralisation of the RIA procedure and the consequent critiques contributed to an institutional void and a lack of legal certainty that led to an increase in the burden of regulation, particularly in the fields of public health, environment and public safety.[32] At the end of the Bush mandate, the US RIA model appeared at once as a pioneering experience worldwide and a problem 'in search of a solution', in strong need of careful redressing, mostly aimed at reducing regulatory burdens for US firms.

1.1.2 RIA under the Clinton Administration

A tentative reaction to this *impasse* was the enactment of Executive Order No. 12,866 in 1993, under the Clinton administration.[33] Within the more general context of 'reinventing government' and the National Performance

---

[30] See Weidenbaum, op. cit.

[31] See e.g. the 1992 Report by the OMB Watch and Public Citizen, *Voodoo Accounting: The Toll of President Bush's Regulatory Moratorium*, stating that claims of huge public savings resulting from the announced regulatory moratorium were hardly substantiated. See also B.D. Friedman, *Regulation in the Reagan-Bush Era: The Eruption of Presidential Influence*. Pittsburgh, PA: Pittsburgh University Press, 1995; and B. Woodward and D.S. Broder, "Quayle's Quest: Curb Rules, Leave 'No Fingerprints'", *Washington Post*, 9 January 1992.

[32] See R.W. Hahn, *Regulatory Reform: Assessing the Government's Numbers*, AEI-Brookings Center for Regulatory Studies, Working Paper No. 99-06, Washington, D.C., July 1999. See also W.F. West, "The Institutionalization of Regulatory Review: Organizational Stability and Responsive Competence at OIRA", *Presidential Studies Quarterly*, No. 1, Center for the Study of the Presidency, Washington, D.C., 2005.

[33] The text of EO 12,866 is available at *http://govinfo.library.unt.edu/npr/library/direct/orders/2646.html* (last visited 5 December 2005).

Review, EO 12,886 attempted to 'cut red tape' by providing OMB with the power to adjudicate conflicts over proposed regulations within a strict 90-day deadline from presentation of the RIA form by the federal agency. If, after the deadline has expired, the conflict between OIRA and the sponsoring agency had not been solved, the President or the Vice-President entered the stage to solve the controversy.[34] The unconditional *veto* power previously awarded to the OMB was then transformed into a conditional opposition with limited potential to infinitely delay entry into force of newly proposed regulations. Furthermore, the Vice-President's power to directly influence administrative policy was replaced with a milder role of 'default' mediator in case the agency and OIRA failed to negotiate a mutually satisfactory solution. This *escamotage* significantly increased the transparency of regulatory reforms in the US.[35]

One of the major problems to be solved was undoubtedly OMB's overwhelming workload in the regulatory review process. Before the Clinton mandate, the OMB, with just 40 employees, had reviewed on average more than 2,200 federal regulations every year.[36] In order to avoid the inevitable inefficiency that followed from such a drastic centralisation, EO 12,866 introduced a minimum threshold, specifying that only regulations whose expected impact was greater than $100 million were

---

[34] See ibid., at section 7: "[t]o the extent permitted by law, disagreements or conflicts between or among agency heads or between OMB and any agency that cannot be resolved by the Administrator of OIRA shall be resolved by the President, or by the Vice President acting at the request of the President, with the relevant agency head (and, as appropriate, other interested government officials)."

[35] *Executive Order 12866: Regulatory Planning and Review*, Federal Register 58, Washington, D.C.: The White House, 30 September 1993. EO 12866 also required that all written communications to OIRA or the White House from non-governmental parties should be placed on the public record. Moreover, the EO ordered that only the OIRA administrator or the deputy administrator could receive oral communications from parties outside the government, and mandated docketing of all conversations between OIRA and agencies as well as between White House officials and private interests.

[36] See, inter alia, the description provided in the OMB's *Report to Congress on the Costs and Benefits of Federal Regulations*, Chapter 1 (available at *http://www.whitehouse.gov/omb/inforeg/chap1.html* – visited 5 December 2005).

subject to mandatory *ex ante* impact assessment.[37] In October 1994, OIRA produced a report entitled "The First Year of Executive Order No. 12866", finding that the number of significant rules reviewed by OIRA had fallen to 900 per year, 60% lower than the 2,200 per year average reviewed under the previous Executive Order, and that about 15% of the rules were found to be 'economically significant'. The report also found that the 90-day review period had been generally respected, and concluded that the new openness and transparency policy had served to defuse, if not eliminate, the criticism of OIRA's regulatory impact analysis and review programme.

1.1.3 RIA under George W. Bush

Although the overall US impact assessment model has remained unchanged since George W. Bush took office, a number of relevant changes have been introduced to the institutional setting of RIA. In particular, these concern the role and powers attributed to the OIRA and the Vice President. As is happening in the EU, the regulatory pendulum in the US shifted patently in the direction of reducing administrative burdens and ensuring least-costly new regulations.

First, EO 13,258, issued on 26 February 2002, removed the Vice President from the regulatory review process.[38] Such removal responded to critiques that hinged on the excessive powers granted to the executive in shaping bureaucrats' decisions, as well as to growing concerns that the involvement of the Vice President could significantly raise procedural costs. At the same time, the Bush administration tried to grant enhanced powers to OIRA. Its structure was consolidated into only four branches – Health, Transportation and General Government; Information Policy and Technology; Natural Resources, Energy and Agriculture; and Statistical and Science Policy. OIRA had six branches in 1992, and five under the

---

[37] More precisely, 'significant regulatory actions' under EO 12,866 rules were those that: i) had an annual effect on the economy of $100 million or more or adversely affect in a material way the economy, a sector of the economy, productivity, competition, jobs, the environment, public health or safety, or State, local, or tribal governments or communities; ii) created a serious inconsistency or otherwise interfered with an action taken or planned by another agency; iii) materially altered the budgetary impact of entitlements, grants, user fees, or loan programmes or the rights and obligations of recipients thereof; or iv) raised novel legal or policy issues arising out of legal mandates, the President's priorities or the principles set forth in EO 12,866.

[38] 67 Federal Register No. 9,385, 2002.

Clinton administration. Such consolidation was aimed at revitalising OIRA, as testified to by its increased staffing level. OIRA had 90 staff members in 1981, but the size had decreased to 69 under Reagan, 60 under Bush Sr. and 47 during the Clinton administration. The George W. Bush administration started out by hiring seven new members and is gradually increasing the staff, hiring also scientists and engineers, and thus bringing skills that OIRA had never had before.[39] OIRA administrator John Graham started issuing 'prompt letters', which suggest that agencies give priority to specific issues – a novelty that was welcomed with enthusiasm by authoritative scholars such as Bob Hahn and Cass Sunstein.[40]

More generally, the removal of the office of the Vice President from its oversight role seems to have led to a more aggressive confrontation between OIRA and federal agencies. Along with some other commentators, the US General Accounting Office remarked that the role played by OIRA vis-à-vis federal agencies has shifted from a 'collaborative, consultative' role under Clinton to that an 'adversarial gatekeeper' model in the Bush administration.[41] Data on the number of rules returned or withdrawn by OIRA confirm this shift. West reports that an annual average of 106 rules were either returned or withdrawn during the last two years of the Bush Sr. administration, whereas the corresponding figure was only 20.5 under Clinton and jumped again to 172 during George W. Bush's first year in office.[42]

OIRA's strengthened role also led to increased attention to standards applied in performing cost-benefit analyses and to a marked reduction in

---

[39] See West, op. cit.

[40] The list of issued 'prompt letters' under the George W. Bush Administration is available at *http://www.whitehouse.gov/omb/inforeg/prompt_letter.html* (visited 5 December 2005). For positive comments on the introduction of prompt letters, see R.W. Hahn and Cass R. Sunstein, *Regulatory Oversight Takes Exciting New Tack*, Working Paper No. 01-25, AEI/Brookings Joint Center Policy for Regulatory Studies, Washington, D.C., September 2001.

[41] See the report by the General Accounting Office on *OMB's Role in the Reviews of Agencies' Draft Rules and the Transparency of these Reviews*, September 2003. See also West (op. cit.), finding that the review has become "less invasive and less confrontational". This new pattern of relationships is sometimes referred to as a 'hot-tub approach', after a definition given by Sally Katzen, Clinton's first OIRA administrator.

[42] See West, op. cit., p. 19.

the estimated dollar cost of new rules. The average annual cost of new rules decreased from $8.5 billion under the first Bush administration to $5.7 billion under Clinton and down to $1.5 billion in the first three years after George W. Bush took office. And, although the total regulatory burden appears to have continued to grow, its growth rate appears to have significantly declined over the past few years.[43] This was also the result of the proliferation of government initiatives on administrative simplification, aimed at streamlining the regulatory environment, facilitating dialogue with small businesses and, more generally, cutting red tape.

1.1.4 US initiatives on administrative simplification

The reform of US RIA, as mentioned above, was not conceived as a stand-alone salvific tool to remedy the mounting burden of US regulatory costs. Already in 1980, Congress responded to the disappointing results contained in the Final Report of the Commission on Federal Paperwork by enacting the *Paperwork Reduction Act* – which required agencies to request OMB approval before collecting information from the public and led to the creation of the OIRA – and the *Regulatory Flexibility Act* – which mandated special analysis of rules affecting small businesses and small governments and created the Chief Counsel for Advocacy as a separate, presidentially appointed officer within the Small Business Administration.[44] In 2001, the House of Representatives passed by a unanimous vote the *Small Business Paperwork Relief Act*, aimed at strengthening the dialogue between the OMB, federal agencies and small businesses, with a specific focus on firms with less than 25 employees. An inter-agency task force was also created, in charge of exploring ways to streamline and consolidate federal paperwork requirements for small businesses. [45]

---

[43] See e.g. the testimony of James L. Gattuso to the Subcommittee on Energy Policy, Natural Resources and Regulatory Affairs Committee on Government Reform, US House of Representatives, on "What is the Bush Administration's Record on Regulatory Reform?", 17 November 2004 (available at *http://www.heritage.org/ Research/Regulation/tst111604a.cfm* – visited 5 December 2005).

[44] See the text of the *1980 Paperwork Reduction Act* at *http://www.thecre.com/pdf/Carter_PaperworkRedAct1980.PDF* (visited 5 December 2005); and the *1980 Regulatory Flexibility Act*, at *http://www.thecre.com/pdf/ Carter_RegFlexAct1980.PDF* (visited 5 December 2005)

[45] See *http://www.sba.gov/advo/laws/hr327_02.pdf* (visited 5 December 2005).

Important steps towards No. 12,866 must be historically contextualised in an era of major reforms, which also affected Congressional activities, until then exempted from external scrutiny. For example, the 1993 *Government Performance and Result Act* (GPRA) required departments to present yearly agendas, which listed prospective regulations, the major goals pursued, the strategies enacted to achieve such goals and all available data on the costs and benefits associated with such proposals.[46] Moreover, the 1995 *Unfunded Mandates Reform Act* (UMRA) prescribed that the Congressional Budget Office provide an estimate of the costs resulting from all new proposed regulations and required federal agencies to identify the preferred regulatory option by following a cost-effectiveness criterion.[47]

But perhaps the most important initiative undertaken during the last two decades is the National Performance Review (NPR) (later named the National Partnership for Reinventing Government), launched in 1993 under the supervision of Vice President Al Gore.[48] The NPR, inspired by the seminal contribution of Osborne and Gaebler, published a report aimed at streamlining and improving the efficiency of federal government activity, which led to cutting as many as 252,000 government jobs in the US administration.[49] The NPR later launched a page-by-page review of existing

---

[46] See *http://www.whitehouse.gov/omb/mgmt-gpra/gplaw2m.html#h1*. The 1993 GPRA set the objective to "improve Federal program effectiveness and public accountability by promoting a new focus on results, service quality, and customer satisfaction".

[47] The text of the *Unfunded Mandates Reform Act of 1995* is available at *http://www.sba.gov/advo/laws/unfund.pdf*. A good example of the attention paid to impact analysis in the US is the commentary to the UMRA published by the Congressional Budget Office, and available at *ftp://ftp.cbo.gov/18xx/doc1891/umra00.pdf* (visited 3 August 2005).

[48] On the experience of the NPR led by Al Gore, see J. Kamensky, *The US Reform Experience: The National Performance Review* (available from the US Government archive at *http://govinfo.library.unt.edu/npr/library/papers/bkgrd/kamensky.html*). The NPR was introduced with the objective of "creating a government that works better and costs less" based on four principles: putting customers first, cutting red tape, empowering employees and cutting back to basics.

[49] On 'reinventing government', see D. Osborne and T. Gaebler, *Reinventing Government: How the Entrepreneurial Spirit is Transforming the Public Sector*, Addison-Wesley Publishing Co., 1992. See also Al Gore, *From Red Tape to Results: Creating a Government that Works Better and Costs Less*, Report of the National Performance

regulation, leading to the identification of 31,000 pages of the federal code to be modified and 16,000 pages to be completely eliminated. [50]

As a result of all these measures, the OMB is now able to publish yearly estimates of the costs and benefits of federal regulation as well as a report on the "Federal information collection burden", which sets yearly burden-reduction targets for individual agencies.[51] Currently, the goal of cutting red tape is the competency of a number of administrative and politically appointed bodies, ranging from the OIRA to the Chief Counsel on Advocacy to the National Ombudsman and individual agency Ombudsmen.[52] Recent attempts to reduce paperwork requirements include technology-driven initiatives such as the creation of the *FirstGov.gov* website, electronic docketing, filing and reporting requirements and the creation of other one-stop shops; the introduction of new time limits for

---

Review, September 1993. The reinventing government approach was recently re-launched in *Positive Outcomes: Raising the Bar on Government Reinvention* by Ted Gaebler, John Blackman, Linda Blessing, Raymond Bruce, Wallace Keene and Paul Smith, Chatelaine Press, 1999.

[50] In his introductory remarks to the *National Performance Review* of 3 March 1993, President Clinton specified that: "Our goal is to make the entire federal government both less expensive and more efficient, and to change the culture of our national bureaucracy away from complacency and entitlement toward initiative and empowerment. We intend to redesign, to reinvent, to reinvigorate the entire national government." The effects of the staff downsizing of US public administration were analysed in detail by the US Office of Personnel Management (available at *http://www.opm.gov/studies/downsize.pdf*).

[51] See OMB, *Report to Congress on Costs and Benefits of Federal Regulations*, op. cit.

[52] Programme Ombudsmen have become widespread in the US administration. In 1990, the Administrative Conference of the US had already issued a recommendation that urged agencies with significant interaction with the public to consider establishing an agency-wide or programme-specific Ombudsman. With the 1993 National Performance Review, the Ombudsman role was promoted throughout federal agencies, for the purpose of increasing public participation in agency proceedings and improving customer service. Currently active programme Ombudsmen include the Small Business Administration Ombudsman, the US Customs Service Trade Ombudsman, the Federal Deposit Insurance Corporation Office of Ombudsman, the Environmental Protection Agency (programme-specific) Ombudsmen, the Food and Drug Agency Office of the Ombudsman and the Security and Exchange Commission's Ombudsman of Municipal Securities. See also OECD, *From Red Tape to Smart Tape. Administrative Simplification in OECD Countries*, Paris, 2003, p. 244.

administrative decision-making, not included in the original text of the *Administrative Procedure Act*, and in a few cases of the 'silent is consent' rule; and the mandatory consideration of alternatives to command and control regulation, with specific emphasis on market-driven, de-regulatory options.

Increased attention on small businesses led to the *Small Business Regulatory Enforcement Fairness Act* (SBREFA), which amended the *Regulatory Flexibility Act* by requiring covered agencies to perform a 'small business impact' test unless the agency head certifies to the Chief Counsel on Advocacy that the proposed rule will not affect a substantial number of small entities. Such certification is published in the *Federal Register* and subject to judicial review. Under the SBREFA, federal agencies are also required to issue guidelines and provide assistance to small businesses in complying with new regulations. Initiatives undertaken for this purpose include the creation of the *RegFair* hotline and website by the Small Business Administration and the appointment of the *US Business Advisor*, a one-stop-shop providing access to Government information, services, and transactions.[53]

Finally, an impressive number of other initiatives are in place to link federal rule-making to individual constituencies and to strengthen dialogue in the advocacy and post-regulatory stage. These include an increased dialogue with standard-setting organisations, the 'tiering' of regulations, the organisation of 'problem-solving days', the creation of the Citizen Advocacy Panel and many others.[54]

1.1.5 The US RIA model

Overall, the new RIA model introduced with EO 12,866 has set a new benchmark for policy-makers worldwide in the field of *ex ante* policy evaluation. This does not mean, however, that RIA sceptics have left the stage. According to some commentators, the rapid transition away from traditional command and control regulation created a shock for US firms, and the comprehensive reform package has not fully met the initial goals. According to others, the OMB, having survived the sharp criticism levelled against it for exercising excessive discretion, today is granted insufficient powers to require agencies to provide a formal demonstration of the

---

[53] Ibid., p. 242. See *www.business.gov* (visited on 30 December 2005).

[54] Ibid., p. 243.

positive impact expected by a new regulation.[55] Finally, the approach adopted by the OMB to cost-benefit analysis was heavily criticised on grounds of being anti-regulatory, non-neutral, overly ambitious and methodologically incorrect.[56]

The institutions that are most heavily involved in the RIA procedure are the proposing agencies and the OIRA. As shown in Figure 1, in the initial stage the proposing agency drafts a preliminary RIA form, comparing different regulatory options – which must include the so-called 'zero option' (leaving the existing regulation unchanged) – and providing a rough estimation of benefits and costs associated with each alternative option and an indication of the relevance of the expected impact of the proposed regulation, which is the *conditio sine qua non* for the activation of the RIA procedure.[57] The RIA form is then subject to a 60-day notice and comment period, in which interested parties can file their comments and suggestions regarding the regulatory option chosen by the agency.[58] After the notice and comment period, the final RIA form is completed as an obligatory step before a final proposal can be drafted and submitted for approval. At this stage, the OIRA has 90 days to approve or reject the proposed regulation on the basis of the quality of cost-benefit analysis performed by the agency. If the proposal is approved, the proceedings go forward. If not, negotiations between OIRA and the proponent agency ensue.

During this second stage, OIRA can call upon its power to reject proposals at will, until the proposal is accompanied by a sufficiently detailed and precise regulatory impact analysis. As recalled in section 1.1.3, the number of rules returned or withdrawn by OIRA has dramatically

---

[55] See, inter alia, R.W. Hahn, J. Burnett, Chan Yee-Ho, E. Mader and P. Moyle, "Assessing Regulatory Impact Analysis: The Failure of Agencies to Comply with Executive Order 12866", *Harvard Journal of Law and Policy*, Vol. 23, No. 3, Summer, 2000.

[56] See Box 2 below in chapter 3, for a more detailed discussion of this critique.

[57] See EO 12,866, op. cit.

[58] The 1946 *Administrative Procedure Act* already recognised the citizen's right to participate in the consultation process. The 60-day notice and comment period was in any event considered only partially satisfactory, as it often results in a mere procedural step, more than a real opportunity to collect valuable views from the general public and targeted groups. See OECD, *The OECD Review of Regulatory Reform in the United States*, OECD, Paris, 1999.

increased under the current Bush administration, as a result of the new 'gatekeeper' role assumed by OIRA after the removal of the Vice President's oversight role.

Figure 1. The US RIA model

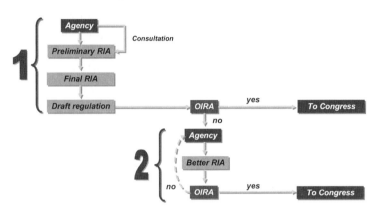

But the oversight activities introduced during the Clinton administration were not limited to Presidential oversight. In 1996, the *Congressional Review Act* prescribed that all sponsoring agencies were bound to send their proposals to the Congress for an evaluation. The US Congressional Budget Office can repeal any draft regulation within 60 days from receipt of the proposal.[59] Such an oversight mechanism also extends to Congressional bills, thus completing the framework of controls over the cost-effectiveness of federal legislation. Nonetheless, a number of commentators have recently advocated the extension of the RIA model to independent agencies.[60] Given the highly 'political' nature of the US RIA model, however, such an extension would significantly undermine the independence of such agencies from the executive.

---

[59] The *Congressional Review Act* is part of the *Small Business Regulatory Enforcement Fairness Act of 1996* (available at *http://usgovinfo.about.com/library/bills/blcra.htm* – last visited 5 December 2005).

[60] See e.g. Gattuso, op. cit.

1.1.6 The US experience: Main lessons for the EU debate

The US impact assessment model is undoubtedly at the forefront of international success stories in policy evaluation. The US is close to being defined as a 'cost-benefit state', with all the advantages and shortcomings that such a definition entails.[61] A close look at the problems that have occurred in the implementation of the US RIA model over the past two decades is of great help in identifying the next steps that may be taken at EU and member state level.

A first lesson to be drawn is related to the *remarkable transparency* of RIA in the United States, thanks also to the public availability of proposals, comments, complaints and communications between OIRA and agencies, and to a massive use of notice and comment procedures, deeply rooted in the US tradition since the end of World War II.[62] Opening the door to mandatory public consultation is, a double-edged sword, as it enables increased participation by the general public in the early stages of the regulatory process, but at the same time exposes regulators to risks of lobbying and capture. This is what occurred in the US following the *Quality of Life Review*, and continued at least until EO 12,866.[63]

An important feature of the US model, that still represents an unattainable frontier – at least in the short run – for EU institutions, is the diffusion of an *evaluation-oriented culture* within US administrations. On the one hand, the conceptual heritage of 'reinventing government' led to a gradual transformation of the US bureaucracy, with the introduction of performance as the ultimate goal of the bureaucrats' visible hand. On the other hand, the unmatched pervasiveness of US RIA enables OMB to publish yearly estimates of the costs and benefits of federal regulation, as mandated by the 1997 *Treasury and Government Appropriations Act*.[64] The yearly publication of estimated costs and benefits of federal regulations

---

[61] For a summary of the current debate on cost-benefit estimates, see Box 2 below. See also C.R. Sunstein, *The Cost-Benefit State*, Working Paper No. 39, University of Chicago Law School, John M. Olin Center for Law and Economics, May 1996.

[62] The public consultation procedure was introduced by the *1946 Administrative Procedure Act*.

[63] For an insightful illustration, see OECD, *The OECD Review of Regulatory Reform in the United States*, Paris, OECD, 1999.

[64] See OECD, *Regulatory Reform in the United States: Government Capacity to Ensure High-Quality Regulation*, OECD, Paris, 1999, p. 10.

certainly fosters the transparency of government regulation, stimulating the political and economic debate.[65]

Another remarkable feature of the US system is the *large number of institutional entities* involved in the regulatory process. While the role played by the Congressional Budget Office complements OIRA's oversight activity, creating an inter-institutional competition that is normally considered virtuous for the quality of regulation, most regulations must pass muster under regulatory flexibility procedures and regulatory burden reduction screens, and are subject to review by an impressive number of constituencies, with specific regard to consumers and small businesses.[66]

Moreover, the US procedure seems to have generated *significant cost savings*. Under the Reagan administration, yearly savings were estimated at roughly $10-20 billion. Non-governmental estimates can however be very different. According to one authoritative economist, the cost of regulations even increased after the introduction of compulsory RIA for federal agencies, and has never stopped mounting since then.[67]

On the other hand, relevant critiques have been addressed to the current implementation of RIA in the US. A 2000 study by Bob Hahn and Bob Litan on 48 proposed regulations subject to RIA between 1996 and 1999 showed that in 27% of the cases agencies had not considered alternative options, and only in 31% of the cases had agencies quantified both expected costs and benefits of proposed regulations. Moreover, only in 63% of the cases had the proponent agency calculated all identified costs, whereas only in 28% of proposals had the agency calculated the net present value of

---

[65] On the reliability of government cost-benefit estimates, see Box 2, chapter 3.

[66] Institutional competition becomes virtuous whenever different entities intervene in the same procedure, but with different and sharply defined roles. In this case, creating a network of competing regulators and oversight agencies produces beneficial effects both in terms of overall transparency and efficiency. See e.g. R. Lutter, *Economic Analysis of Regulation in the U.S.: What Lessons for the European Commission?*, AEI-Brookings Joint Center for Regulatory Studies, Washington, D.C., 2001.

[67] R.W. Hahn and R. Litan, *An Analysis of the Third Government Report on the Benefits and Costs of Federal Regulation*, AEI-Brookings Joint Center for Regulatory Studies, Washington, D.C., 2000; and E.A. Posner, "Controlling Agencies with Cost-benefit Analysis: A Positive Political Theory Perspective", *University of Chicago Law Review*, Vol. 68, 2001.

the regulatory intervention.[68] More recently, in 2004 Bob Hahn and Pat Dudley analysed 55 cases of RIA performed by federal agencies between the Reagan, Bush Sr. and Clinton administrations, with similar results.[69] Accordingly, economists have stressed the need for further improvements in the accuracy of cost-benefit estimates by federal agencies as a necessary measure for improving the quality of *ex ante* evaluation. Robert Hahn and Robert Litan have also issued recommendations on how to improve the quality of US RIA, by enhancing the soundness and pervasiveness of the model.[70]

Furthermore, besides critiques addressed towards the quality of RIAs performed by federal agencies, some disagreement has emerged as regards the scope of application of the US RIA model. As of today, the US impact assessment procedure only involves federal agencies, not independent authorities, i.e. the authorities that normally deal with the most relevant part of economic regulations.[71] And, while it is certainly true that such authorities ought to be left independent of the executive, many commentators have criticised the decision to limit the application of RIA scrutiny to all new rules except core economic and social rules enacted by giant regulators, such as the FCC (Federal Communications Commission), the FTC (Free Trade Commission) or the SEC (Securities and Exchange Commission).[72]

---

[68] Ibid.

[69] R.W. Hahn and P. Dudley, *How well does the government do cost-benefit analysis?*, Working Paper 04-01, AEI-Brookings Joint Center for Regulatory Studies, Washington, D.C., January 2004.

[70] See R.W. Hahn and R.E. Litan, "Counting Regulatory Benefits and Costs: Lessons for the U.S. and Europe", *Journal of International Economic Law*, Vol. 8, No. 2, 2005, pp. 473-508 (see in particular pp. 496-499, suggesting that "Congress pass a law requiring that *all* federal regulatory agencies submit annual cost and benefit estimates of major regulations to OMB", and that "OMB issue a scorecard assessing the overall quality of regulation and ask the agencies to complete a scorecard for each major regulation").

[71] R.W. Hahn and C. Sunstein, "New Executive Order For Improving Federal Regulation? Deeper and Wider Cost-Benefit Analysis", *University of Pennsylvania Law Review*, Vol. 150, No. 1489, May 2002; T.O. McGarity, "Regulatory Analysis and Regulatory Reform", *Texas Law Review*, Vol. 65, No. 1243, 1987. See also R.H. Pildes and C.R. Sunstein, "Reinventing the Regulatory State", *University of Chicago Law Review*, 62, 1, 1995.

[72] See e.g. congressional testimony by James L. Gattuso, op. cit.

Finally, the US regulatory review model has been the subject of extensive study by game theorists and political scientists, as its peculiar institutional setting lends itself to applications of principal-agent models and raises issues of political control over the bureaucracy.[73] For example, Lazer (2004) finds evidence that, although the staff at OIRA has remained quite stable between Bush Sr. and Clinton administrations, the White House has radically redistributed its attention and political support towards OIRA members with compatible political viewpoints. The appointment of John Graham as the OIRA head and the gradual strengthening of OIRA's role as gatekeeper are seen as consistent with the removal of the Vice President from the review procedure, a solution aimed at ensuring that the White House keeps control over federal agencies and at the same time economising on its fairly limited capacity to gather information on proposed new rules.

This finding is compatible with a competitive agent model of control, and suggests that, in the regulatory review model adopted in the US, presidential influence is exerted mostly through an institutionalisation of the conflict and competition between the anti-regulatory OIRA and activist regulatory agencies, such as the Environmental Protection Agency or the Occupational Safety and Health Administration. In this model, the President has a clear incentive to exert heavy control on the bureaucracy also because the White House competes with the Congress in controlling bureaucrats.[74]

---

[73] See, inter alia, T. Moe, "Regulatory performance and presidential administration", *American Journal of Political Science*, 26(2), pp. 197-224, 1982; T. Moe, "Control and feedback in economic regulation: The case of the NLRB", *American Political Science Review*, 79, 1985, pp. 1094-1016; T. Moe, "The new economics of organization", *American Journal of Political Science*, 79, pp. 1094-1117. See also William A. Niskanen, *Bureaucracy and Representative Government*, Chicago, IL: Aldine, 1971.

[74] See D. Lazer, *Regulatory Review: Presidential Control through Selective Communication and Institutionalized Conflict*, 1998 (available at *http://www.ksg.harvard.edu/prg/lazer/control.pdf* – visited 5 December 2005).

1.2 The UK experience: From 'light touch' to 'limited touch' regulation

The UK experience on impact assessment is starkly different from that in the US, and can be considered as the expression of Europe's 'state of the art' as well as a possible reference model for the past and current EU impact assessment models. Compared to the US model, the UK model exhibits peculiar features, mostly related to: i) the choice to provide for a gradual introduction of the procedure; ii) the peculiar attention to compliance costs borne by target firms; iii) a strong emphasis on the impact of regulation on small and medium-sized firms; and iv) the type of regulations that are subject to impact assessment (in the US proposed regulations by federal agencies, in the UK draft bills presented to the Parliament).

The first attempts to introduce a culture of impact assessment and an *ex ante* evaluation of the expected impact of proposals examined by the Parliament can be traced back to the Thatcher administration. The UK Government, however, decided to proceed with caution, initially mandating only a simplified procedure, which entailed that sponsoring administrations estimated only the impact of proposed legislation on the costs borne by firms to comply with the new rules (so-called 'Compliance Cost Assessment' or CCA). The CCA procedure, introduced in 1986, clearly aimed at reducing administrative burdens that were found to be skyrocketing – just as in most other EU countries – as a result of regulatory creep.[75] The slogans used at that time – such as 'building businesses – not barriers' and 'lifting the burden' were self-explanatory.[76]

The introduction of CCA must be contextualised within the more general reform of UK public administration that led, during the early 1980s, to a true, disruptive cultural revolution in UK administration, transforming a procedure-oriented bureaucracy into a more performance-oriented, efficiency-driven branch of the government. The so-called 'new public management' wave led to a significant improvement in the efficiency of the UK administration, achieved through a reform of contractual arrangements with CEOs, but also through a growing use of market-type mechanisms (MTMs), an increased outsourcing of functions inefficiently performed by

---

[75] See R. Boden, J. Froud, A. Ogus and P. Stubbs, *Controlling the Regulators*, London: MacMillan Press, 1998.

[76] See the White Paper, *Lifting the Burden*, Cmnd 9751, 1985; and *Building Business – Not Barriers*, Cmnd 9794, 1986.

the state and more generally though stronger emphasis on performance and citizens' satisfaction in the delivery of public services.[77]

The UK CCA model relied heavily on the coordination and oversight of an *ad hoc* government task force, whose main role was to coordinate 'anti-red tape' initiatives and to assist sponsoring administrations in drafting CCA forms. In 1986, following the 'Building businesses – not barriers' initiative, the agency was given the name of Enterprise and Deregulation Unit and was nested in the Department of Employment. In 1987 it was renamed the Deregulation Unit and moved to the Department of Trade and Industry, where it was assisted by a task force of business representatives. The Deregulation Unit conducted its activities in an 'adversarial, inquisitorial' way, challenging administrations by setting ambitious yearly targets for the reduction of administrative burdens, paving the way for a massive deregulatory effort. In 1992, most departments had gone a long way towards reducing regulatory creep, but the real target of reducing administrative burdens seem not to have been achieved.[78] Commentators and politicians highlighted that a further cultural shift was needed in UK administrations in order to drive the process of cutting red tape and facilitating business activities. The 'new wave' of reforms launched in 1992 maintained the same 'gatekeeper' model and led to the creation of new *ad hoc*, sector-specific bodies similar to the US federal agencies. Seven new task forces were created in 1992 alone – including a Deregulation Task Force – for the purpose of facilitating the deregulation initiative launched by John Major's administration. These task forces spawned as many as 605 deregulatory initiatives, which led, inter alia, to: i) the *1994 Deregulation and Contracting Out Act*, which introduced legislative means to abrogate regulatory burdens; ii) the 'think small first' initiative, which forced administrations to award top priority to the impact

---

[77] For an illustration of the 'new public management' approach, see Jan Erik Lane, *New Public Management*, London: Routledge, 2000; and Christopher Pollitt and Geert Bouckaert, *Public Management Reform. A Comparative Analysis*, Oxford: Oxford University Press, 2000. The approach survived the 1980s and 1990s and is still considered to provide significant guidance for policy-makers in the modernisation of government. See e.g. OECD, *Modernising Government: The Way Forward*, Paris, 2005, p. 85 and p. 181.

[78] See OECD, *From Red Tape to Smart Tape*, op. cit., p. 197.

of existing and new regulations on small enterprises; and iii) the extension of CCA to parliamentary bills and EC directives.[79]

However, evidence soon testified that these huge efforts were producing only little progress in alleviating compliance costs. When the DTI moved to the Cabinet Office in 1995, a new initiative was launched for improving the overall UK regulatory environment for businesses. Departments were asked to issue monthly reports on their planned legislative activities and were warned not to use 'gold-plating' of EC directives, especially after the unfortunate experience in the transposition of the Data Protection Directive.[80] Moreover, in 1996 the CCA procedure was gradually transformed into a wider 'regulatory appraisal', which included risk assessment and the requirement to quantify benefits as well as costs.[81]

Only in 1998, under the Blair premiership, a real Regulatory Impact Assessment procedure was introduced, based on a thorough analysis of costs and benefits of identified regulatory options, including the 'zero option'. According to the UK Cabinet Office, the new RIA procedure will allow future yearly savings up to £100 million. This would certainly be a remarkable result, although there is still no empirical evidence available to confirm such estimates.[82] Again, this new wave of reforms was accompanied by a thorough restatement of the role and functions of UK administration. The White Paper on *Modernising Government* marked the final shift from an input-oriented to an outcome-oriented approach to delivery of public service.[83] Greater attention was devoted to the simplification of the regulatory environment, with the creation of the Small Business Service and the Panel for Regulatory Accountability within the Cabinet Office. Likewise, in 2000 the Deregulation Unit was heavily reformed in its composition and main functions, and renamed the Regulatory Impact Unit (RIU). Regulatory impact units were also created at

---

[79] Ibid., p. 198.

[80] See e.g. the Report by the Better Regulation Task Force, *Simplifying EU Law*, December 2004, p. 18 (available at *http://www.brtf.gov.uk/docs/pdf/simplebetter.pdf* – visited 5 December 2005).

[81] See, inter alia, the House of Commons Research Paper No. 04/52, *Small Firms: Red Tape*, 28 June 2004.

[82] See *http://www.cabinet-office.gov.uk*.

[83] See Tony Blair and Jack Cunningham, *Modernising Government*, White Paper, March 1999.

departmental level. The RIU's 'Scrutiny Team' became a cross-departmental task force and adopted a more collaborative approach vis-à-vis administrations, with an eye to helping them develop a stronger culture of evaluation and cost-effectiveness.[84]

The internal structure of the RIU became more articulated at the end of the 1990s. In 1997, a Better Regulation Task Force (BRTF) was created within the RIU, replacing the Deregulation Task Force as an independent advisory group with a strong representation from businesses, consumers and the voluntary sector.[85] The BRTF must advise the Government by ensuring that proposed regulations are "necessary, fair and affordable", as well as simple to understand and administer. Besides advising the Government, the BRTF also advises departments at an early stage of drafting, by issuing non-coercive recommendations. But perhaps the most important role played by the BRTF lies in the drafting of guidelines and documents on methodological issues. Starting in 2000, the BRTF published reports on the impact of regulation on small firms in specific sectors (e.g. the IT sector, the hotel/catering sector, etc.). In 2003, the task force began to identify best practices in regulatory impact assessment (the so-called 'champions of better regulation'), bringing them to the attention of the National Audit Office.[86] Most notably, the BRTF issued in 1998 and updated in 2000 and 2003 a list of 'principles of good regulation', which specifies that regulation and its enforcement should be proportionate, accountable, consistent, transparent and targeted.[87] Starting in 2002, the BRTF issued specific guidance on methodological issues, by recommending the adoption of non-regulatory alternatives;[88] combating regulatory

---

[84] See OECD, *From Red Tape to Smart Tape*, op. cit., p. 201.

[85] See the BRTF's website (*http://www.brtf.gov.uk*).

[86] See the BRTF' Annual Report 2001/2002, *Champions of Better Regulation* (available at *http://www.brtf.gov.uk/docs/pdf/ar2002.pdf* – visited 5 December 2005). In April 2002, the Committee of Public Accounts recommended that the National Audit Office undertake annual evaluations of a sample of RIAs. See the NAO reports, *Evaluation of Regulatory Impact Assessments Compendium Report 2003-04* (HC 358 Session 2003-04), 4 March 2004; and *Evaluation of Regulatory Impact Assessments Compendium Report 2003-04* (HC 341 Session 2004-2005), 17 March 2005.

[87] See the Principles of Good Regulation (available at *http://www.brtf.gov.uk/reports/principlesentry.asp* – visited 5 December 2005).

[88] See BRTF, *Alternatives to State Regulation*, July 2000 (available at *http://www.brtf.gov.uk/docs/pdf/stateregulation.pdf* – visited 5 December 2005).

inflation;[89] and streamlining legislation.[90] The importance of the work carried out by the BRTF is also testified to by the recent document on the use of consultation at EU level.[91] The BRTF also relied on voluntary measures such as the Enforcement Concordat, a non-statutory code designed to ensure that central and local enforcement agencies developed a more proportionate approach to regulatory enforcement. By December 2001, 96% of local authorities and the vast majority of central agencies had voluntarily adhered to the prescriptions of the Concordat.[92]

Finally, the BRTF also developed a "test of good regulation and pitfalls to be avoided" which applies to all available regulatory options (state and non-state regulation). The BRFT suggests that administrations make sure that proposed initiatives have broad political support; are enforceable and easy to understand; are balanced and avoid "impetuous knee-jerk reactions"; avoid unintended consequences; balance risk, costs and practical benefits; seek to reconcile contradictory policy objectives; and identify accountability issues.[93]

The valuable contribution from the BRTF was incorporated in the RIU Guide to regulatory impact assessment, published in 2000 and then revised and updated in 2003.[94] The Guide included a detailed illustration of the criteria to be followed in performing cost-benefit analysis. Sponsoring administrations now can rely on insightful documents, which include specific guidance on alternatives to state regulation, including "regulation

---

[89] See BRTF, *Avoiding Regulatory Creep*, October 2004 (available at *http://www.brtf.gov.uk/docs/pdf/hiddenmenace.pdf* – visited 5 December 2005).

[90] See BRTF, *Make it Simple Make it Better – Simplifying EU Law*, December 2004 (available at *http://www.brtf.gov.uk/docs/pdf/simplebetter.pdf*); and *Regulation – Less is More. Reducing Burdens, Improving Outcomes*, March 2005 (available at *http://www.brtf.gov.uk/docs/pdf/lessismore.pdf*).

[91] See *Get Connected – Effective Engagement in the EU*, September 2005 (available at *http://www.brtf.gov.uk/docs/pdf/getconnected.pdf* – visited 5 December 2005).

[92] See the DTI Website at *http://www.dti.gov.uk/ccp/topics1/enforcement.htm#retailpilot*; and also OECD, *From Red Tape to Smart Tape*, op. cit., p. 212. According to the Concordat, enforcement should be based on standards, be open, consistent, proportional and helpful, offer a widely published and timely complaint procedure, and offer opportunity for consultation.

[93] See the BRTF 'Test' at *http://www.brtf.gov.uk/docs/pdf/principlesleaflet.pdf*.

[94] See BRTF, *Good Policy-Making: A guide to regulatory impact assessment*, London, Cabinet Office, 1999.

through information", regulation through codes of practice, self-regulation, deregulatory options, market-based options, etc.

1.2.1 The 2001 Regulatory Reform Act and the 2002 Regulatory Reform Action Plan

Notwithstanding the proliferation of initiatives aimed at promoting better regulation, the ambitious plans formulated by the UK government after 1998 did not fully materialise. Administrations still lacked sufficient awareness of the need to enact cost-reducing regulations and to ease regulatory burdens, and the growth of the regulatory burden seemed not to have slowed down. Furthermore, the Parliament exhibited a lack of legislative capacity, with specific respect to the transposition of EU directives. New initiatives were thus undertaken to address the issue of reforming existing legislation, with specific emphasis on simplifying procedural steps towards the revision of legislation currently in force, by granting the Government enhanced powers to intervene in existing primary and secondary legislation.

A first attempt to establish fast tracks to lift the burden of already existing primary and secondary legislation had been made with the 1994 *Deregulation and Contracting Out Act*. The Act enabled the Government to make a Deregulation Order (DO) to amend or repeal a provision in primary legislation that was considered to impose a burden on businesses or others or could be reduced or eliminated without removing any necessary protection. The results, however, were quite disappointing: during the 1995-96 Session, 19 proposed Deregulation Orders were submitted before the Parliament, but the number decreased to 12 in 1996-97 and to five in the 1997-98 Session. The following year, only four proposed DOs reached the Parliament, highlighting the need for releasing some of the overly restrictive limits set by the 1994 Act on the scope of governmental power to tackle regulatory burdens.[95]

The stark disappointment with the limited outcome of the 1994 Act led to a wide consultation launched by the Cabinet Office in 1999. In the paper entitled "Proposed Amendments to the Deregulation and Contracting Out Act of 1994", published in March 1999, the Cabinet Office stated that it was "possible to extend the scope of the power to fulfil its

---

[95] See OECD, *From Red Tape to Smart Tape*, op. cit., p. 211, and the House of Commons Second Special Report of the Deregulation Committee, 16 May 2000.

commitment to modernise government and deliver regulatory arrangements appropriate for the years to come". After a tough negotiation between the Government and the Parliament, agreement was reached on the need to reform and widen the Government's order-making power.

Such an extensive negotiation process eventually led to the approval of the Regulatory Reform Act, which came into force on 1 April 2001, enabling ministers to amend or repeal laws in order to lift regulatory burdens through a streamlined approach which entailed, inter alia, the removal of 'double-banking', aimed at simplifying Parliament procedures. More importantly, for the purpose of this paper, the 2001 Act addressed the persistent lack of standardised procedures for reviewing existing legislation. A RIA-like procedure was mandated for the review of existing legislation, ensuring further Parliamentary scrutiny of Government proposals for regulatory review through a special procedure (called the 'super-affirmative' procedure), in which the Regulatory Reform Orders (RROs, which replaced the Deregulation Orders) are subject to public consultation and then to a detailed scrutiny by the Regulatory Reform Committee in the House of Commons and the Delegated Powers and Regulatory Reform Committee in the House of Lords.[96]

Under the 2001 Act, the RROs can serve a number of different purposes, including: i) making and re-enacting statutory provisions; ii) imposing additional burdens provided they are proportionate; iii) removing inconsistencies and anomalies in legislation; iv) dealing with burdens caused by a lack of statutory provision to do something; v) applying RIA to all legislation that has not been amended in substance during the last two years; vi) relieving burdens from anyone, except government departments where only they would benefit; and vii) allowing administrative and minor details to be further amended by subordinate provisions orders.[97]

After the entry into force of the 2001 Act, encouraging outcomes started to emerge. At the end of 2003, more than 240 deregulatory measures

---

[96] See the House of Commons Second Special Report of the Deregulation Committee, 16 May 2000, §§27 ff. (available at *http://www.publications.parliament.uk/pa/cm199900/cmselect/cmdereg/488/48804.htm* – last visited 5 December 2005).

[97] The Act also empowers the government to produce a code of good enforcement practices. Its main intention is to provide safeguards against potential problems linked to the use of the voluntary approach to the Enforcement Concordat. See OECD, *From Red Tape to Smart Tape*, op. cit., p. 211.

had already been delivered with the new RRO system. Some of these produced significant outcomes: for example, licensing reforms, including increased flexibility over opening hours, are expected to save roughly £1.9 billion in the first 10 years of implementation; reforms to business tenancies had the potential to save "approximately £6.5 million a year in court costs alone"; and the removal of limits to the number of partners in a firm was estimated to save around £10,000 per relevant partnership.[98] Provisions aimed at lifting the burden on small firms included measures that raised the audit threshold from £1 to £5.6 million (which freed 69,000 businesses) and the introduction of a flat rate scheme that saved 672,000 small businesses from having to complete detailed VAT returns. As regards the simplification of Parliament procedures, the UK reached out into the seven countries that met the target for 98.5% on-time transposition of EU directives. Studies by KPMG, the World Bank and OECD ranked the UK as the most competitive regulatory environment, with specific regard to regulatory costs.[99] But in 2005, evidence gathered during the so-called 'Hampton review' revealed that small businesses were still faced with disproportionate regulatory burdens.[100] This led the UK Government to a decision not to raise the flag on better regulation, but instead to proceed with new, more ambitious initiatives.

1.2.2 Latest developments: The 2005 Action Plan and the creation of the Better Regulation Executive

The past few years were dominated by a re-launch of UK initiatives on cutting red tape and reducing regulatory creep for small businesses. These include a number of administrative simplification initiatives, mostly linked to the e-Government initiatives and one-stop-shops created at central and agency level (such as the portal *Ukonline.gov*, the *info4local* and *Small*

---

[98] See the updated *Regulatory Reform: the Government's Action Plan*, published on 10 December 2003, and available at *http://www.cabinetoffice.gov.uk/regulation/ documents/regulatory_reform/pdf/ rrap2003.pdf* (last visited 5 December 2005).

[99] See KPMG, *The CEO's Guide to International Business Costs*, 2004; OECD, *Economic Survey of the United Kingdom*, Paris, March 2004; and World Bank, *Doing Business in 2005: Understanding Regulation*, Washington, D.C., September 2004.

[100] See P. Hampton, *Reducing Administrative Burdens: Effective Inspection and Enforcement*, December 2004 (available at *http://www.hm-treasury.gov.uk/media/935/ 64/Hampton_Interim_Report_709.pdf* – last visited 2 August 2005).

Business Service initiatives).[101] The 2002 Regulatory Reform Action Plan was updated in 2003.[102] The number of Regulatory Reform Orders scrutinised by the Parliament skyrocketed, creating further need for stronger methodological requirements and Government oversight. For this reason, a number of important initiatives were undertaken to increase the internal consistency of such a complex reform endeavour.

First, in June 2005, the Chancellor of the Exchequer, Gordon Brown, launched a new, ambitious Better Regulation Action Plan. The Action Plan announced the introduction of a 'quite different' appraisal model, aimed at embedding the risk-based approach in regulatory decision-making. The risk-based approach was announced as providing for "no inspection without justification, no form filling without justification, and no information requirements without justification."[103] The Action Plan followed the publication of the "Less is More" paper by the BRTF, as well as the Hampton Review on administrative burdens, which had suggested the adoption of a risk-based approach as well as massive consolidation of UK regulators. As a result, Chancellor Brown announced the plan to reduce UK regulators from 31 to as few as seven.[104] The plan, included in the forthcoming *Better Regulation* bill currently under consultation, will be finalised and implemented in September 2006.

Under the prescriptions of the Action Plan, Departments will start measuring the total administrative burden they impose upon businesses (including the costs of form-filling, undergoing inspections and complying with data requirements).[105] Moreover, businesses will be invited to propose areas of regulation and administrative costs that are needlessly burdensome, also through a brand new online portal (accessed at *www.betterregulation.gov.uk*). The Panel for Regulatory Accountability within the Cabinet Office will be in charge of setting challenging targets for burden reduction for each department by the 2006 pre-budget report. In early 2006, departments will have to start preparing 'simplification plans'

---

[101] For a detailed description of the e-Government initiatives undertaken in the UK over the past few years, see OECD, *From Red Tape to Smart Tape*, op. cit., p. 204.

[102] See Cabinet Office, *Regulatory Reform: The Government's Action Plan*, op. cit.

[103] See e.g. "Brown Pledged to Cut Business Red Tape", *The Guardian*, 24 May 2005.

[104] See Cabinet Office, *A Bill for Better Regulation: A Consultation Document*, 25 July 2005, chapter 2.

[105] See the press release of the Cabinet Office, "Cabinet Office kicks-off project to measure and cut red tape on business", CAB 043/05, 15 September 2005.

by reviewing existing legislation and taking into due account proposals coming from businesses as well as guidelines contained in the Hampton review and in the BRTF's "Less is More" document.[106]

In particular, the 'Better Regulation' bill will mandate new fast tracks for repealing or amending outdated and unnecessary legislation, set out the powers to merge regulatory bodies and introduce new tools aimed at promoting the use of a risk-based approach as recommended during the Hampton review. After the consultation period expires, the bill will be introduced to Parliament in early 2006 and will be subject to Parliamentary approval. Its entry into force is scheduled for summer 2006. Detailed deregulatory proposals – mostly based on suggestions by businesses – will then be included in a further 'Deregulation' bill to be submitted to Parliament by the second session of 2006.[107]

But there's more in the new 2005 Action Plan. For example, a new Local Authority Better Regulation Group is being set up, comprising local authorities, national regulators and government departments, "to improve the coordination of local and national regulatory services". In order to establish a common approach to risk assessment and regulatory best practice, authorities will agree on a national Regulatory Enforcement Concordat, whose first draft will be published in autumn 2005. The Department of Trade and Industry already started a consultation on a new Consumer and Trading Standards Agency, in charge of developing a single code of practice to replace and harmonise the 203 trading standards offices currently active nationwide, thus reducing differences in the quality and consistency of regulation experienced by businesses with multiple locations.

---

[106] As stated in the Treasury's Press Notice of 24 May 2005, "Chancellor launches Better Regulation Action Plan": "Regulators prepare for legislative changes by beginning to join-up their enforcement practices in 'shadow' form, and starting to implement the risk-based approach recommended by Hampton. In particular they begin to: a) reallocate their resources to areas where the regulatory risk is greatest, reducing the burden on compliant businesses and enhancing regulatory outcomes overall; b) perform more joint inspections, determined by proper assessment of risk, so that there is no inspection without a reason; and c) reduce data requirements on business, by designing shorter forms and sharing more information." See also BRTF, *Less is More*, op. cit.

[107] See Cabinet Office, *A Bill for Better Regulation*, op. cit.

Most importantly, the new Action Plan also specified the priorities to be pursued by the UK Presidency of the European Union. These include advocating the introduction and correct implementation of comprehensive impact assessment at EU level, as well as methods to estimate clearly and transparently the administrative burdens imposed by EU proposals on businesses. The UK Government also planned to develop a list of priorities for simplifying the EU regulatory environment, and drafted a timetable for delivering regulatory simplification in 2006. Finally, the UK Government plans to promote the use of the new risk-based approach also at EU level.[108]

But the Action Plan also paved the way for a thorough reassessment of the whole RIA model adopted in the UK. The appointment of John Hutton, Chancellor of the Duchy of Lancaster, as Cabinet-level minister led to replacing the RIU with a Better Regulation Executive (BRE), in charge of: i) providing stronger central coordination of delivery and implementation of the Hampton review as well as the 'make it simple-make it better' and the 'less is more' recommendations from the BRTF; ii) supporting the Panel for Regulatory Accountability as 'gatekeeper', challenging departments in case of insufficient progress towards regulatory reform; and iii) acting as 'consultant' to departments for the purpose of enabling cultural change and more outcome-oriented processes.[109]

In launching the consultation phase on the new Better Regulation Bill on 20 July 2005, the Government announced that it had accepted all eight recommendations issued by the BRTF in the "Less is More" report, and decided to focus on the following three main objectives:

- regulating only where necessary and with a light touch that is proportionate to risk,
- setting exacting targets for reducing the cost of administering regulations and
- rationalising the inspection and enforcement arrangements for both business and the public sector.

The Action Plan also announced that in January 2006 the BRTF will be replaced with a new Better Regulation Commission, whose main role will be to advise and challenge government departments on regulatory reform issues and to scrutinise departmental plans for regulatory simplification.

---

[108] See the Press Notice, "Cabinet Office kicks-off project", op. cit.

[109] See the Better Regulation Executive Website (*www.cabinetoffice.gov.uk/regulation*).

Finally, by the end of 2006, the National Audit Office will start reporting to the Parliament on departments' performance in implementing the new risk-based methodology and in effectively reducing the burden of regulation, as well as on regulators' performance against the recommendations of the Hampton Review.[110]

As clearly emerges from this brief explanation of the main features of the new Action Plan, the institutional setting of UK Better Regulation is set to be constantly changing and will significantly depart in the next two years from the model adopted up to 2004. As recalled by Sir John Hutton in launching the consultation on the new *Better Regulation Bill*, "[t]he potential economic gains from stripping away unnecessary regulation are enormous". Hutton also recalled estimates by the BRTF that the new approach "could boost British national income in the long term by 1% of GDP – a huge gain of around £10 billion for the UK economy".[111] The BRTF also calculated that adopting the standard cost model already adopted in the Netherlands (SCM) for measuring administrative burdens and then targeting a 25% cut in such burdens over four years could reduce direct regulatory costs on businesses by £7.5 billion, yielding a £16 billion increase in the UK GDP in the medium term.[112]

---

[110] See, again, the Cabinet Office's press notice, "Cabinet Office kicks-off project", op. cit., and the Cabinet Office's Consultation Document, *A Bill for Better Regulation*, op. cit.

[111] See the Cabinet Office's press notice, "Transforming the Regulatory Landscape – Launch of a Consultation on a Bill for Better Regulation" (available at *http://www.cabinetoffice.gov.uk/regulation/news/2005/050720_bill.asp* – visited 5 December 2005). The approach taken by the UK Government has been termed 'one in, one out', to express the need to "encourage a better balance between the introduction of new regulation and deregulation". See speech by Sir David Arculus, Chairman of the Better Regulation Task Force, to staff of the Financial Services Authority, 29 June 2005 (available at *http://www.fsa.gov.uk/Pages/Library/Communication/Speeches/2005/0705_sda.shtml* – visited 5 December 2005).

[112] See the Statistical Appendix to the *Less is More* White Paper (available at *http://www.brtf.gov.uk/pressreleases/2005/lessismore.asp#stats* – visited 5 December 2005).

1.2.3 The UK RIA model

Figure 2 shows the RIA model adopted by the UK government. As is easily seen, the procedure is essentially composed of two stages.[113] In the first stage, the proponent administration performs an initial regulatory impact assessment, identifying the range of alternative regulatory options available for solving the specific issue at hand. The initial RIA form also carries an identification of the preferred regulatory option. Such form is then filed with the competent ministry, which decides whether to proceed in the drafting of the proposed new regulation. The RIA form then is sent back to the proponent administration, whose task is now to identify the most appropriate methodology for the type of regulation at stake (for example, cost-effectiveness analysis, compliance cost assessment, cost-benefit analysis, risk-risk analysis, etc.).[114] The choice of the methodology is made in consultation with RIU (now BRE) and the Small Business Service, created for the purpose of representing the interests of small and medium-sized enterprises as targets of new regulations.

At this stage, the proposed regulation is sent again to the Ministry, which is required to verify whether the proposal meets the thresholds for a Regulatory Impact Assessment Statement (RIAS), a detailed RIA whose completion is mandatory only if the expected impact is greater than £20 million; when the issue is of particular interest to the general public; or when the proposal is likely to exert a biased impact on different social groups.

The BRE takes part also in this process, and collaborates with the sponsoring administration in drafting the RIAS. The result of this process is the publication of the so-called 'partial RIA', followed by a consultation process and inter-departmental dialogue. As a matter of fact, in the UK experience, RIA is part of a wider process in which the proposed regulation is filed with the Prime Minister through the Cabinet Office. The proposal will be handed back to the competent minister with attached comments and guidelines on the methodology to be used for impact assessment and on actions to be undertaken for solving the regulatory issue at stake. Only

---

[113] See RIU, *Better Policy-Making: A Guide to Regulatory Impact Assessment*, op. cit.

[114] For an illustration of methodologies currently used in the UK RIA model, see the Treasury's *Green Book: Appraisal and Evaluation in Central Government*, updated in 2003 (available at *http://www.hm-treasury.gov.uk/media/05553/Green_Book_03.pdf* – visited 5 December 2005).

when the final RIA form is drafted, such form is signed by the minister and sent to the Parliament for discussion and approval.

Figure 2. The UK RIA model

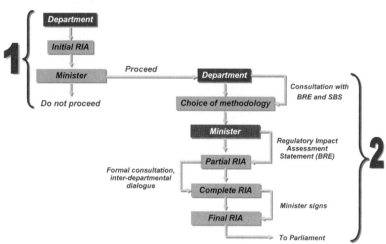

1.2.4 Main lessons from the UK experience

The UK RIA experience surely ranks amongst the most advanced best practices and constitutes an example of insightful practical implementation of a policy tool that has so far seldom kept the promise of significantly enhancing the quality of regulation. However, not all that glitters is gold: the huge effort devoted by UK administrations in refining the RIA procedure has so far produced only limited visible improvements in the efficiency and accountability of the UK regulatory process, as testified to by the constant overlapping of initiatives launched by the Cabinet Office, always in search of new organisational arrangements and methodological refinements in its RIA procedure.

Amongst the most evident virtues of the UK model, as already recalled, is certainly the choice to gradually introduce complex RIA tools, with no resort to trial stages in which administrations are immediately called to adopt overly complex procedures in a restricted sample of selected proposals. The complexity of the UK RIA model has increased over time, as administrations became more familiar with the new organisational culture imposed by the 'new public management' revolution. The application of the economic theory of organisation, which inspired the whole new public management movement, allowed for a thorough understanding of the importance of cultural change as a key driver for an efficient transition towards a better performance in public administrations, efficient organisational behaviour and, in turn, better regulatory processes.[115] The UK bureaucracy had the time to become familiar with the tools of economic analysis needed for assessing the costs and benefits of regulation, which normally are not part of the standard endowment of the 'Weberian-style' bureaucrat.

Moreover, the UK experience must be appreciated for its attention to principles of good regulation. According to the guidelines of the Better Regulation Task Force, which were accepted and endorsed by the Cabinet Office, proposed bills must be proportionate, consistent, targeted, transparent and accountable. Proportionality implies that regulators should intervene only when necessary, that regulations must be appropriate to the risks posed and that costs associated with regulations have to be identified and consequently minimised. The principle of proportionality also includes a careful scrutiny of the impact of proposed regulations on small businesses, which are estimated to account for 99.8% of UK businesses.[116] The 'think small first' principle was first developed in the UK and was adopted at EU level as early as the 1980s.

The targeting principle is also particularly important. The Better Regulation Task Force has mandated regulators to focus on the problem and minimise side effects, thus avoiding a scattergun approach. The approach to regulation must be clearly 'goals-based' and flexible, with room for consultation between regulators and targeted groups. Furthermore, an emphasis on compliance costs still remains in the

---

[115] The initial stage of UK RIA was characterised by a strong emphasis on cultural change as a key driver of better regulation. The Thatcher administration even started distributing economics and public choice materials to senior public officials, in order to raise their awareness and stimulate performance-oriented behaviour. See N. Bosanquet, "Sir Keith's Reading List", *Political Quarterly*, 52(3), 1983, pp. 324-341.

[116] See BRTF, *Better Policy-Making: A Guide to Regulatory Impact Assessment*, op. cit.

principles of good regulation, which specify that "those being regulated should be given the time and support to comply".[117]

Finally, it is worth noting that at least some administrations in the UK have reached a significant level of accuracy in estimating the costs and benefits of proposed regulations as well as in the drafting of RIA forms, although the Chairman of the Better Regulation Task Force, David Arculus, recently reported to the National Audit Office (NAO) that stark differences exist between agencies that perform RIA quite well (e.g. the Department of Trade and Industry) and administrations that produce poor quality estimates (the Home Office, the Department of Transport and the Department of Culture, Media and Sport).[118]

In addition, the UK model has been heavily criticised for not taking adequately into account goals other than the economic efficiency of proposed regulations.[119] In particular, the application of cost-benefit analysis to proposals with strong expected social impact might lead to neglecting important objectives for policy-makers, such as safety, social justice or fairness. Three objections must be put forward in this respect, however. First, the new RIA procedure still maintains a strong emphasis on protecting small businesses, an objective that seems at least partially inconsistent with the mere search for economic efficiency.[120] Secondly, RIA is always presented as a tool that may help regulators, with no ambition to become a panacea for policy-making or to entirely replace the 'art' of

---

[117] See e.g. *Better Regulation: Making Good Use of Regulatory Impact Assessments – A Report by the Comptroller and the Auditor General*, 15 November 2001 (available at *http://www.nao.org.uk/publications/nao_reports/01-02/0102329.pdf* – visited 5 December 2005). The five principles of good regulation (transparency, proportionality, targeting, consistency and accountability) were introduced by the Better Regulation Task Force in 1997 and then updated in 2000 and 2003. See also *Principles of Good Regulation* (available at *http://www.brtf.gov.uk/docs/pdf/principlesleaflet.pdf* - last visited 7 December 2005).

[118] See the National Audit Office reports on RIAs at *http://www.nao.org.uk/ria/index.htm*, and the Letter to the Comptroller General of BRTF Chairman David Arculus of 26 May 2005 (available at *http://www.brtf.gov.uk/docs/pdf/sir_john_letter_26may05.pdf*), requesting further scrutiny of RIAs by the NAO.

[119] See OECD, *UK Regulatory Reform: Challenges at the Cutting Edge*, Paris, 2002.

[120] The 'Small Business (Litmus) Test' is performed by individual sponsoring administrations in collaboration with the Small Business Service, created by the Labour administration in 2000 with the specific aim to cut small business red tape.

regulation with the 'craft' of cost-benefit analysis. Thirdly, individual sectoral agencies such as the Office of Communications (OFCOM), Office of Gas and Electricity Markets (OFGEM) and the FSA (Financial Services Authority) started developing ad hoc RIA methodologies, submitting them to public consultation. Such an initiative will arguably foster the introduction of more specific tools in an otherwise standardised assessment model.[121]

Finally, as already recalled, it must be added that the cost-saving and efficiency-enhancing potential of the RIA model is still not confirmed by any empirical evidence. According to some commentators, the 'gold-plating' approach adopted in transposing some EC directives into national law caused an undesirable increase in administrative burdens and other regulatory costs in a number of cases.[122] This is also made dependent on the absence of a thorough assessment of all the regulatory options available to the regulator. Cases of 'costly' adoption of EU legislation include the transposition of the Data Protection Directive (95/46/EC) into national law with the *Data Protection Act* of 1998. The adoption of the EU framework led – according to estimates by the UK chambers of commerce – to a 50% increase in business compliance costs. Such experience led Whitehall to consider issuing ad hoc guidelines for the adoption of EU legislation, which recently culminated in the distribution of a 'Transposition Guide' drafted by the RIU and of the 'Make it simple make it better' list of recommendations by the Better Regulation Task Force.[123]

---

[121] See section 3.3 below.

[122] See BRTF, *Make it Simple Make it Better*, op. cit.

[123] The Regulatory Impact Unit or RIU (now renamed Better Regulation Executive) devoted peculiar attention to the transposition of EU legislation. Major publications on this topic are the *Transposition Guide: How to Implement European Directives Effectively* (available at *http://www.cabinet-office.gov.uk/regulation/docs/europe/pdf/tpguide.pdf*); *Better Policy-Making: A Guide to Regulatory Impact Assessment* (available at *http://www.cabinet-office.gov.uk/regulation/docs/europe/pdf/tpguide.pdf*); *Better Policy-Making: Checklist to Ensure Good Quality European Legislation* (available at *http://www.cabinet-office.gov.uk/regulation/docs/europe/pdf/tpguide.pdf*); and, finally, the *Report on Improving UK Handling of European Legislation* (available at *http://www.cabinetoffice.gov.uk/regulation/documents/europe/pdf/euchecklist.pdf* – last visited 7 December 2005).

1.3   EU impact assessment: Panacea or Pandora's box?

The European Commission has adopted methods for assessing the impact of its regulations since 1986, when the Business Impact Assessment (BIA) System was launched under the UK Presidency. The BIA system, like the UK Compliance Cost Assessment procedure, exhibited a strong focus on the impact of proposed regulations on business enterprises, with no specific emphasis on social welfare as a whole. As such, the BIA procedure elicited strong criticisms for its lack of theoretical soundness and minimal impact on the regulatory costs faced by European firms.[124] For this reason, such a system was gradually integrated with an array of initiatives and projects (such as the Business Test Panel, the SLIM project, etc.), aimed at extending the limited scope of the BIA. Such a hysteresis of initiatives ended up creating an overly confused scenario for EU impact assessment – exactly the regulatory creep that impact assessment was supposed to counter. For this reason, the EU institutions in 2002 agreed on the need for new action in the field of better regulation, with a specific focus on impact assessment.

Today, as EU policy-makers are striving to lead Europe away from its disappointing economic performance and back onto the Lisbon track, better regulation has become a new mantra, and the *ex ante* impact assessment of EU legislation is conquering new fans, who see it as the philosopher's stone that will improve the quality of EU legislation in the years to come. Thus, better regulation strongly relies on the successful implementation of the ambitious new Integrated Impact Assessment (IIA) model, which entered into force on 1 January 2003 and mandated the assessment of the economic,

---

[124] See, inter alia, the Final Report Business Impact Assessment (BIA) pilot project, *Lessons Learned and the Way Forward*, Enterprise Paper No. 9, DG Enterprise, European Commission, 2002, p. 2. The Commission acknowledged that BIA "has not always worked as originally intended … Instead, BIAs are often carried out as an *ex-post* 'paper exercise' on already finalised proposals, leading to significant drawbacks with regard to both the quality of the analysis made and the possibility of feeding the results into the drafting process". The Final Report also mentioned that "many BIAs are not backed up by objective information and impacts on business are rarely quantified", and that "[t]here is little evidence of an institutional learning process from previous BIAs". The report is available at *http://europa.eu.int/comm/enterprise/library/enterprise-papers/pdf/enterprise_paper_09_2002.pdf* – visited 5 December 2005).

social and environmental impact of major new initiatives included in the Annual Policy Strategy or in the annual Legislative Work Programme.

A growing emphasis on impact assessment is found in the 2003 Inter-Institutional Agreement on Better Regulation, in the Parliament's 'Doorn Motion', in the Joint Statement issued on December 2004 by six consecutive Council Presidencies on "Advancing Regulatory Reform" and in the Commission's Communication on Better Regulation for Growth and Jobs in the European Union, issued in March 2005. And *ex ante* impact assessment is now being extended to major amendments proposed by the Council and the Parliament within co-decision procedures. Even at the recent US-EU summit held in Washington, D.C. on 20 June 2005, impact assessment was constantly in the spotlight, and the next summit will call for closer transatlantic cooperation on regulatory issues.[125]

So far, so good. But is all this enthusiasm justified? Behind the façade, two decades of experience in OECD countries have highlighted that impact assessment is far from being a panacea, especially when it is built on shaky methodological and organisational grounds. 'Bad' impact assessment can raise administrative costs, increase regulatory creep, facilitate regulatory capture and lead to suboptimal regulations. Accordingly, EU policy-makers will be able to reap the benefits of better regulation only when the integrated impact assessment (IIA) model reaches more satisfactory standards from a methodological, organisational and institutional perspective.

The next sections are dedicated to an illustration of the initiatives undertaken at EU level for the purpose of promoting high-quality regulation through *ex ante* impact assessment over the past two decades. Chapter 2 focuses on the current scorecard of the Commission DGs in performing regulatory impact assessment. Chapter 3 explores 10 roadmaps conceived for the purpose of reconciling – to the extent possible – the *sein* and the *sollen* of the EU impact assessment model in the near future.

---

[125] See e.g. the speech by European Commissioner Viviane Reding, announcing "an OMB-European Commission dialogue to address, subject to mutual agreement, topics such as good regulatory practices, transparency provisions and public consultation, impact assessment methodologies and risk assessment methodologies", as well as the creation of a "High Level Regulatory Co-operation Forum to promote regulatory cooperation between senior regulators". See her speech 05-446, Washington, D.C., 13 July 2005.

1.3.1 The early years: The BIA system

The EU experience in regulatory impact assessment began in 1986, when the UK took its turn in the Presidency of the Council. For this reason, the impact analysis procedure introduced – called Business Impact Assessment (BIA) – closely echoed the UK model of Compliance Cost Assessment.[126] The BIA Pilot Project aimed at evaluating the impact of a limited number of proposed regulations on businesses, expressed in terms of compliance costs. Since 1989, the procedure has been put under the competency of DGXXIII (DG Enterprise), which coordinated other DGs and selected the proposals included in the Commission's agenda that should be subjected to a BIA test.[127] The BIA Pilot Project led to a selection of draft proposals from DG Enterprise in the fields of detergents, electromagnetic compatibility, environmental impact of electrical and electronic equipment (EEE) and prepackaging, and concentrated on examining three major elements of the impact assessment process, namely external consultation, economic analysis and organisational structures.

Figure 3 illustrates the essential structure and the critical steps of the BIA procedure. As shown in the figure, DG Enterprise ensured that a limited number of proposals included in the Annual Policy Strategy were scrutinised under the BIA procedure. If a proposal was found to exert a substantial impact on compliance costs, the sponsoring administration was required to draft a *fiche d'impact*. The *fiche* had a standard form, and was introduced with the aim of representing the likely impact of the proposal at hand on target firms. First, the *fiche* illustrated the main reasons for intervention. Lead DGs were asked to explain the reasons for changing legislation currently in force (or to intervene *ex novo* in unregulated fields). The next step was the identification of businesses that would be affected by the proposed intervention, followed by a list of actions to be undertaken in order to comply with the changing regulatory environment. For each of these actions a cost estimate had to be provided, by specifying bureaucratic costs, taxes, monitoring and reporting costs and other compliance costs.

---

[126] See section 1.2.1 above.

[127] See the BIA Final Report, op. cit.

Figure 3. The BIA procedure

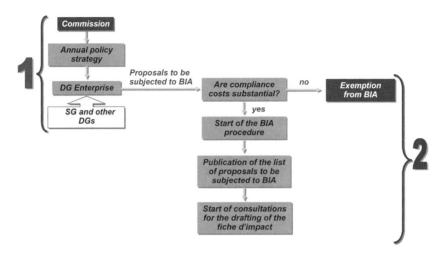

The standard *fiche d'impact* also included an evaluation of the likely macroeconomic effects of the proposed regulation, which in turn incorporated the impact on employment and on the investments and competitiveness of target firms. Finally, the *fiche* should devote specific attention to assessing the expected impact of the proposal on SMEs, in line with the established 'think small first' principle.[128] While drafting the *fiche*, lead DGs were required to consult interested stakeholders. The final document contained a summary of the opinions expressed during the consultation process.

The BIA system was subject to heavy criticism, mostly related to its incompleteness and uncertain institutional setting. Firstly, as was already mentioned, the BIA procedure did not imply the preliminary identification of a range of alternative regulatory options, and only entered the stage after the Commission had identified the preferred option in its yearly regulatory agenda. Secondly, the BIA only contained information on business compliance costs, without considering other cost categories or the social impact of the proposed regulation, often less easily quantifiable and rarely

---

[128] The 'think small first' principle was included in the European Charter for Small Enterprises, as endorsed by the Heads of State or Government at the Santa Maria da Feira European Council of 19-20 June 2000 (Annex III of the conclusions of the Santa Maria da Feira European Council).

subject to market exchange. Furthermore, the EU experience with BIA was characterised by the scant scientific soundness of the evaluations performed, which cast heavy doubts on the reliability of such instrument as a support to EU policy-makers.[129] The absence of training initiatives for officials of the DGs in charge of BIA contributed further to generate a widespread sense of pessimism over the prospects for improving the quality of performed evaluations in the short run without changing the procedure completely.[130]

For this reason, the Commission decided during the 1990s to add new tools and to launch new projects for the purpose of completing the evaluation of proposals carried out under the BIA system. Such initiatives include the SLIM project (Simplification of the Legislation on the Internal Market), aimed at strengthening the *ex post* assessment of the quality of regulation; the creation of the BEST (Business Environment Simplification Task Force) in 1997; and the creation of the Business Test Panel in 1998, with the aim of acting as a permanent body for consultation of firms affected by EU regulations.[131]

Such a proliferation of initiatives, however, did not produce the desired outcome, and ended up creating an overly fragmented framework for EU impact assessment. This led the Commission to issue in 2001 a White Paper on European Governance and the Lisbon Council to mandate the creation of a high-level advisory group (the 'Mandelkern Group') for the drafting of an "action plan for better regulation" and the definition of a new model of impact assessment to be implemented at Community level. The Mandelkern Group was created to "set out by 2001 a strategy for further co-ordinated action to simplify the regulatory environment,

---

[129] See the BIA Final Report, op. cit.

[130] Ibid., p. 23, stating the need for a 'cultural change', both within the institution and in its relationships with the public, through the implementation of a series of straightforward and common-sense adjustments, which are intended to be neither bureaucratic nor complicated to put in place.

[131] As regards the SLIM pilot project, see the Commission Communication of 6 November 1996, COM(96)559 (available at *http://europa.eu.int/comm/internal_market/ simplification/docs/com1996-559/com1996-559_en.pdf* – visited 5 December 2005). The subsequent Commission reports are available at *http://europa.eu.int/comm/ internal_market/simplification/index_en.htm#slim* (visited 5 December 2005). For what concerns the BEST project, the Final Report, issued in May 1998, is available at *http://europa.eu.int/comm/enterprise/enterprise_policy/best* (visited 5 December 2005).

including the performance of public administration, at both national and Community level", and after the Ministers for Public Administration from EU members states had signed the Strasbourg Resolution in November 2000, mandating the advisory group to "develop a coherent approach to this topic and to submit proposals to the Ministers, including the definition of a common method of evaluating the quality of regulation."

Such model was expected to provide a more complete tool for assessing the social, economic and environmental impact of proposed regulations.[132]

1.3.2 The 2001 White Paper and the Mandelkern Report

The Commission's 2001 White Paper on European Governance clarified the Commission's agenda for the establishment of new better regulation standards in the EU.[133] The preparation of the White Paper was coordinated by the former 'Governance team' chaired by Jerome Vignon. The team organised 12 working groups dealing with six main working areas. Working Group 2c dealt with issues of better regulation and explored possible actions for improving the quality of regulation at EU level as well as the implementation of EU legislation at member state level. Better regulation was defined in terms of seven dimensions, namely proportionality, proximity, legal certainty, coherence, high standards, timeliness and enforceability. The need for action at member state level was stressed during the preparatory work for the White Paper, in stating that "action at Community level alone – and a fortiori by the Commission alone – is certain not to succeed".[134] Subsequent developments, unfortunately, confirmed such prophecy.

---

[132] The Mandelkern Group was made up of representatives of the EU-15 and officials from the Commission's Secretariat-General. An interim report was finalised at the end of February 2001 and considered by the Heads of State and Government at the Spring European Council in Stockholm. The Final Report (so-called 'Mandelkern Report') was published in November 2001; the majority of recommendations were included in the Commission's 2002 Better Regulation Action Plan.

[133] See European Commission, White Paper on European Governance, COM(2001)727, 25 July 2001.

[134] See the Preparatory Work for the White Paper, European Commission, 2002, p. 119 (available at http://europa.eu.int/comm/governance/areas/preparatory_work_en.pdf (visited on December 7, 2005).

According to Working Group 2c, BIA was an inadequate tool to appraise the expected impact of a regulation for a number of reasons. First, BIA was "only a questionnaire, without a proper process and without guidance".[135] This, according to the opinion expressed by the working group, could lead to significant differences in the quality of the analysis. Moreover, the questions were handled only at a late stage of the regulatory process, when political pressures are expected to be highest.

Finally, BIA was found to be inappropriate since the analysis contained in the *fiche* was presented separately from the tests of subsidiarity and proportionality and the sectoral provisions in the Treaty, leaving stakeholders and policy-makers unaware of the relationship between prospective costs arising from the proposal for businesses and expected benefits to consumers, the environment or SMEs. Accordingly, more sophisticated tools were needed in order to support policy-makers with clearer, more relevant and more comprehensive information on the prospective cost/benefit balance of regulatory proposals.[136]

The preparatory report of the working group on evaluation and policy also recommended the use of cost-benefit analysis as the most complete and accurate methodology in the evaluation of proposed legislations.[137] However, exact economic calculations were considered not to be the most important contributors to regulatory quality. Rather, the working group took a 'lesson-drawing' approach by stating that observing the international experience and undertaking contextualised benchmarking are the most important steps towards a compete understanding of the logic of decision-making. The working group also suggested that monitoring existing EU legislation was at least as important as evaluating the expected impact of new regulation.[138]

The publication of the White Paper on European Governance was followed by a fierce debate and a period of frantic institutional tension. The European Parliament issued a resolution on governance in the wake of the 'Kaufmann Report', in which it criticised the lack of cooperation between the Commission and the Parliament in defining the EU agenda for better

---

[135] Ibid., p. 106.

[136] See e.g. J. Pelkmans, S. Labory and G. Majone, op. cit.

[137] See Preparatory Work for the White Paper, op. cit., section 3.2.1, p. 91.

[138] Ibid., section 3.3.3, p. 92.

regulation.[139] In other words, the Parliament complained that, after stating the need for cooperation at both horizontal (inter-institutional) and vertical (with member states) level, in fact the Commission was 'playing solo' on the reform of European governance. For such reason, the Parliament warned the Commission "against taking measures in the legislative sphere which might affect the roles of Parliament and the Council in the legislative process before Parliament has been fully consulted".[140] Instead, the resolution suggested the promotion of stronger inter-institutional dialogue on governance reform, and welcomed the establishment of an inter-institutional working group announced by President Romano Prodi on 2 October 2001.

But the Parliament resolution contained other interesting comments on the Commission's White Paper. In particular, the Parliament considered some of the plans formulated by the Commission in the White Paper as patently (and sometimes unnecessarily) ambitious. Instruments such as "online consultation through the inter-active policy-making initiative" (Section 3.1 of the White Paper) created, in the Parliament's view, the "risk of an escalation in consultation" which would end up being incompatible with the Commission's goal of "reducing the long delays associated with the adoption and implementation of Community rules".[141]

A few months after the publication of the White Paper on European Governance, the Mandelkern Group on Better Regulation published its final report. The report specified some of the features of the prospective new RIA model, suggesting its adoption by the Commission before June 2002 and its application to all Commission proposals with possible regulatory effects.[142] The Mandelkern Group also recommended that the Council and the Parliament should not consider proposals that had not been subjected to the agreed impact assessment system, except in cases of

---

[139] European Parliament, *Report on the Commission White Paper on European Governance*, A5-0399/2001, adopted by the European Parliament on 29 November 2001 (OJ C 153E, 27 June 2002, pp. 314-322).

[140] Ibid., p. 8.

[141] Ibid., p. 8.

[142] Mandelkern Group, Final Report (available at *http://europa.eu.int/comm/ secretariat_general/impact/docs/mandelkern.pdf* – visited 5 December 2005).

urgency.[143] Furthermore, the Mandelkern Report highlighted the need for increased participation by member states at an early stage of preparation of proposals, as well as the need for each member state to adopt its own impact assessment system "adapted to their circumstances" by June 2003.

As regards Regulatory Impact Assessment (RIA), the Mandelkern Report contained a set of recommendations for an effective implementation of such procedure. These included the following steps:[144]

- description of the problem or risk to be addressed;
- description of different options considered;
- listing of the affected parties and at least a qualitative assessment of impact on them;
- summary of the consultation process undertaken and of its results;
- estimation of the lifetime of the policy or options;
- description of the impact on SMEs or other disproportionately affected group;
- explanation of how the proposal fits with existing rules and policies; and
- description of the methodology adopted.

The Mandelkern Group also recommended the adoption of a 'dual stage' RIA model, with a preliminary impact assessment devoted to the analysis of alternative regulatory options and an extended impact assessment in which the detailed assessment of the benefits and costs of the preferred regulatory option is performed.

However, the Mandelkern Report did not contain any indication on the scope and comprehensiveness of the impact to be assessed. The recommendations following from the Final Report represented a fairly important input into the Commission's new impact assessment model. But, as will be clearer in the next section, the Commission's new Better Regulation Action Plan and the Communication on impact assessment, both issued in June 2002, went somehow further than what the high-level advisory group had envisaged.

---

[143] On 30 September 2002, the Competitiveness Council stated its intention, in principle, not to consider substantial regulatory proposals that were not accompanied by proportionate impact assessments.

[144] See the Mandelkern Report, op. cit., p. 26.

1.3.3 Away from RIA: Building the Integrated Impact Assessment

At the European Council meetings of Göteborg and Laeken, the Commission announced its Action Plan for Better Regulation, launched in June 2002. The new impact assessment model was introduced as part of the wider Action Plan, together with a communication aimed at simplifying and improving the regulatory environment and measures aimed at promoting "a culture of dialogue and participation" within the EU legislative process (see Box 1).

Box 1. Elements of the Action Plan for Better Regulation

During 2002 and early in 2003, the Commission developed its Action Plan through eight targeted Communications, at the same time defining with the European Parliament and the Council an overall strategy on better law-making. The Communications addressed the following issues:

1) General principles and minimum standards for consultation (COM(2002)704);
2) Collection and use of expertise (COM(2002) 713);
3) Impact assessment (COM(2002) 276), including internal *Guidelines*;
4) Simplifying and improving the regulatory environment (COM(2002) 278);
5) Proposal for a new comitology decision (COM(2002) 719);
6) Operating framework for the European Regulatory Agencies (COM(2002) 718);
7) Framework for target-based tripartite contracts (COM(2002) 709); and
8) Better monitoring of the application of community law (COM(2002) 725).

The Communication on impact assessment was inspired partially from the activity of the Mandelkern Group, but also from the commitment undertaken by the Commission at the Göteborg Council, to develop a tool for sustainable impact assessment.[145] As a result, the Commission decided to integrate all forms of *ex ante* evaluation by building an integrated impact assessment model, to enter into force on 1 January 2003.[146] Such model

---

[145] See Communication COM(2002)276, p. 2. See also the Communication from the Commission to the European parliament, the Council, the Economic and Social Committee and the Committee of the Regions, *Towards a Global Partnership for Sustainable Development*, COM(2002)82, 12 February 2002.

[146] "Impact assessment is intended to integrate, reinforce, streamline and replace all the existing separate impact assessment mechanisms for Commission proposals."

bears the heavy responsibility of ensuring that adequate account is taken at an early stage of the regulatory process of both the competitiveness and sustainable development goals, which rank amongst the top priorities in the EU agenda.

The new integrated impact assessment (IIA) model introduced in 2002 – which incorporates not only the economic impact, but also the social and environmental impact of the proposals concerned – adopts a 'dual stage' approach. All Commission initiatives proposed for inclusion in the Annual Policy Strategy or the Commission Legislative and Work Programme and requiring some regulatory measure for their implementation – thus including not only regulations and directives, but also white papers, expenditure programmes and negotiating guidelines for the international agreements – must undergo a 'preliminary impact assessment'.[147] Moreover, a selected number of proposals with large expected impact, are subjected to a more in-depth analysis called 'extended impact assessment'.

The selection of proposals for extended impact assessment forms part of the Commission programming and planning cycle. On the basis of the preliminary impact assessment statement, the Commission decides in the Annual Policy Strategy or (later) in its annual Legislative and Work Programme which proposals should undergo an extended impact assessment. In making this decision, it takes into account whether the proposal will result in substantial economic, environmental and/or social impacts on a specific sector or several sectors; whether the proposal will have a significant impact on major interested parties; and whether the proposal represents a major policy reform in one or several sectors.

See the Commission's Communication on impact assessment, COM(2002) 276, 5 June 2002, section 1.3.

[147] Proposals that are exempted from impact assessment include: i) green papers where the policy formulation is still in process; ii) periodic Commission decisions and reports; iii) proposals following international obligations; iv) executive decisions, such as "implementing decisions, statutory decisions and technical updates, including adaptations to technical progress"; and v) Commission measures deriving from its powers of controlling the correct implementation of Community Law (although the Commission may in some instances decide to carry out an impact assessment). See Communication on impact assessment, COM(2002) 276, 5 June 2002, section 2 ("Coverage").

The preliminary impact assessment consists of a short statement containing an identification of the issue at stake, the regulatory options available (including the 'zero option' or 'no policy change' scenario), preliminary indications on the expected impact and an indication of whether an extended impact assessment would be needed. There is no clear identification of the policy option to be preferred, but only a specification of the options that should be excluded at the preliminary stage, taking into account also the subsidiarity and the proportionality principle. Overall, the outline for preliminary impact assessment does not seem to be particularly informative.

The extended impact assessment (ExIA) contains an in-depth evaluation of the expected social, economic and environmental impact of the various policy options associated with the proposal and a summary of the consultation activity, which should also focus on political and ethical issues related to the proposal. The Commission also specified that the expected impact should be estimated in qualitative, quantitative and possibly monetary terms. The alternative policy options are to be evaluated according to criteria such as the relevance to the problem, the effectiveness in achieving the objectives, the coherence with wider economic, social and environmental objectives, the interaction with other existing and planned Community interventions, the cost or resources required and the user-friendliness of the regulatory option at hand.

More in detail, the Commission provides a description of what is meant by economic, social and environmental impact:

- The *economic* impact includes both the macro- and micro-economic impact of the selected option, mostly in terms of economic growth and competitiveness, i.e. changes in compliance costs, including administrative burdens to businesses/SMEs and implementation costs for public authorities, impacts on the potential for innovation and technological development, changes in investment, market shares and trade patterns as well as increases or decreases in consumer prices, etc.

- The *social* impact includes the impact of the proposal on human capital, on fundamental/human rights, the compatibility of the proposal with the Charter of Fundamental Rights of the European Union, but also prospective changes in employment levels or job quality, changes affecting gender equality, social exclusion and poverty, impacts on health, safety, consumer rights, social capital, security (including crime and terrorism), education, training and culture, as well as distributional implications such as effects on the income of particular sectors, groups of consumers or workers, etc.

- The *environmental* dimension concerns positive and negative impacts associated with the changing status of the environment such as climate change, air, water and soil pollution, land-use change and bio-diversity loss, changes in public health, etc.

As clearly emerges from these definitions, the IIA model proposed by the Commission appears as a complex exercise, aimed at predicting all possible consequences of the enactment of a new regulation, with evaluations that – whether qualitative or quantitative – will certainly be costly, burdensome, highly discretionary and time-consuming for administrations. Furthermore, the often denounced lack of training for EU public officials, which led to obscure and unreliable assessments at a time when the BIA was the prevailing impact assessment tool, will certainly create far greater problems with entry into force of such a new procedure, whose complexity goes probably beyond that of any other impact assessment model implemented worldwide. It must be recalled that the Commission decided to introduce the new procedure gradually, and expected to reach the planned complexity and comprehensiveness only in 2004. Moreover, in September 2002, the Commission published its guidelines for the implementation of an impact assessment procedure.

The new IIA model introduced by the Commission in 2002 is illustrated in Figure 4. As emerges from the diagram, the new procedure permeates the whole Commission's Strategic Planning and Programming Cycle (SPPC), from the definition of the Annual Policy Strategy (APS) to the publication of the Commission's Work Programme (CWP) that leads to inter-service consultation before selected initiatives are undertaken and pursued. Preliminary IAs can be included in the APS, but must be completed at the latest before the publication of the CWP. The availability of an extended IA (for proposals that have been selected for it) is a necessary precondition for launching inter-service consultation at the beginning of the year in which the regulation will be issued. The ExIA report is then attached to the proposal when it is submitted to the Commission for final adoption and is adopted as a working document of the services. After adoption, the ExIA is sent to the other institutions along with the proposals and made available on the web.

Figure 4. IIA in the Commission's SPPC

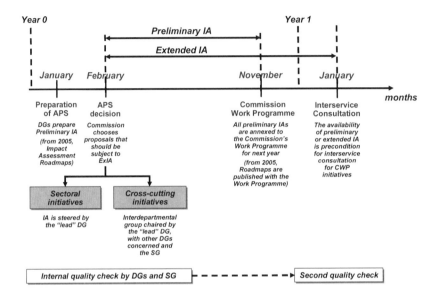

2. Putting EU Integrated Impact Assessment into Practice

At first blush, the new integrated impact assessment model appeared to adequately take into account the main lessons drawn from international best practices in regulatory impact assessment, in particular from the UK and US experiences described in the previous sections. From a theoretical standpoint, the new EU model seems more complete and effective than its UK and US counterparts, since it integrates the features of regulatory impact assessment, sustainable impact assessment and other types of *ex ante* policy evaluation. However, the procedure appeared from the very beginning as being overly complex and likely to generate excessive administrative and transaction costs, given, inter alia, the need to coordinate the activity of many directorates-general and the General Secretariat; the uncertain boundaries of consultation; the absence of clear guidelines on the implementation of the proportionality principle; and many other sources of uncertainty for administrations, which in turn still lacked sufficient training and expertise. As a matter of fact, no major effort has been actually made in this respect, notwithstanding the resounding appeals by the Parliament and the Council in the Kaufmann and the Mandelkern Reports.

Against this backdrop, it is hardly surprising that a number of difficulties have emerged during the first two years of implementation, ranging from organisational problems (institutional conflict of competencies, excessive transaction costs, principal-agent incentive issues, asymmetric information on the side of EU regulators, exposure to third-party capture of EU regulators) to theoretical problems (insufficient proportionality, lack of flexibility, limited consultation, insufficient training of the Commission's employees, slow cultural change within EU institutions in charge of carrying out RIA); and methodological problems (insufficient assessment of environmental and social impact, difficulties in choosing the inter-temporal discount rate, incomplete cost-benefit analysis, failure to quantify costs and/or benefits, etc.).

This sensation was confirmed by available data on the procedure's first trial year. In its Work Programme for 2003, the Commission had planned to have 43 extended RIAs completed by the end of the year, representing roughly 20% of the Commission's total number of initiatives subject to RIA under the new model. However, only 22 of the foreseen 43 Impact Assessment procedures were completed in 2003. The low implementation rate was at once cause and effect of a number of teething problems, which the Commission is now. trying to tackle. First, the assessment of the environmental and social impacts of the proposals needs to be fully developed. Secondly, extended impact assessments should include a more thorough discussion of the principles of subsidiarity and proportionality, in particular of the respective merit of different regulatory approaches. Thirdly, analyses tend to focus on one policy option. Policy alternatives should be examined more thoroughly. Fourthly, there has been so far limited quantification, let alone monetisation, of the impacts. Fifthly, efforts should be undertaken to make RIAs more accessible to the general public. Sixthly, the application of this new model seems to have imposed quite a heavy burden on EU administrations, increasing the cost of many regulations. Finally, and most importantly, the new RIA model does not apply to regulations upheld by individual member states. Initiatives aimed at facilitating the convergence/coordination of national impact assessment procedures may therefore be highly advisable in order to improve the regulatory process and foster both competitiveness and sustainable development.[148]

Similar conclusions were drawn by the Commission in the progress report on the implementation of the new IIA model, published on 21 October 2004.[149] The Commission highlighted that the principle of proportionality had not been adequately implemented, leading to overly burdensome procedures. According to the Commission, "[w]hile initial

---

[148] See also N. Lee and C. Kirkpatrick, *A Pilot Study of the Quality of European Commission Extended Impact Assessments*, IARC Working Paper Series No. 8, Impact Assessment Research Centre, University of Manchester, 2004 (available at *http://idpm.man.ac.uk/iarc/Reports/IARCWP8.DOC.pdf*).

[149] See European Commission Staff Working Paper, *Impact Assessment: Next Steps - in Support of Competitiveness and Sustainable Development*, SEC(2004)1377, Brussels 21 October 2004.

experience shows that the methodology used is sound, there needs to be a more systematic application of the current methodology across Commission services. When applied correctly, the current method addresses many of the points raised by Council and Parliament as needing more emphasis, including coverage of impacts in all three dimensions – economic, environmental and social. The Commission notes, however, that the generalised use of Impact Assessments cannot be considered neutral either from the point of view of resource allocations or as regards the programming cycle of the EU's legislative process. The complexity of a sizable number of Impact Assessments is therefore likely to require longer preparatory phases before their approval."[150]

Furthermore, scholars that have undertaken a tentative assessment of the first IIAs undertaken by European Commission DGs have reported quite puzzling results. For example, Lee and Kirkpatrick scrutinised the first six ExIAs completed by the Commission in 2003, reporting a number of weaknesses and an overall heterogeneity in the quality of the assessment performed. Methodological weaknesses included an unclear description of the problem, obscure ranking of the objectives, a relatively narrow range of alternative policy options considered, an unbalanced coverage of different types of impact (e.g. economic, social, environmental), unreliable assessment findings, deficiencies in the presentation of report findings, insufficient time and resources available to complete a sufficiently detailed analysis, lack of transparency in the process and inadequate arrangements for external consultation.[151]

Similarly, Vibert (2004) analysed the first 20 Extended IAs performed by the Commission, by applying a scorecard approach similar to that developed by Robert Hahn of the AEI/Brookings Center for Regulatory Studies in the US.[152] The results are quite disappointing: out of 20 Extended

---

[150] Ibid., p. 4.

[151] See Lee and Kirkpatrick, op. cit., p. 27.

[152] F. Vibert, *The EU's New System of Regulatory Impact Assessment – A Scorecard*, European Policy Forum, London, 2004. See also Robert W. Hahn and Patrick M. Dudley, *How Well Does the Government Do Cost-Benefit Analysis?*, Working Paper No. 04-01, AEI-Brookings Joint Center for Regulatory Studies, Washington, D.C., January 2004; and, for a recent comparison of scorecards for US and EU, Robert W. Hahn and Robert E. Litan, "Counting Regulatory Benefits and Costs: Lessons for the U.S. and Europe", *Journal of International Economic Law*, Vol. 8, No. 2, 2005, pp. 473-508.

IAs, only 10 quantified (and only 9 monetised) costs and benefits, only 11 carried data on market alternatives and only 2 contained a provision for peer review. Finally, all 20 proposal subjected to IA were finally approved, and 10 were re-designed as a consequence of the results obtained in the IIA process. The author concluded that the EU IIA model deserves a positive initial evaluation, in particular because it added a lesson-learning dimension to the formulation of the Commission's legislative initiatives. However, it must be noted that the unreliability and heterogeneity of the cost-benefit analysis severely undermines the actual contribution that the new procedure can provide to EU competitiveness and sustainable development in the medium range.

Other scorecards are provided by two recent studies. Opoku and Jordan (2004) analyse all of the 41 ExIAs completed by lead DGs in 2003 and 2004, by focusing in particular on the consideration of the external dimension and on the detailed scoring of a more limited set of ExIAs, related to the sugar regime, the tobacco regime, the REACH Directive, the Kyoto Protocol, the 'Youth in Action' programme and the 'Lifelong learning' programme. They conclude that a number of measures would be required to improve the consideration of the external dimension in ExIAs. These include "updating the guidelines with more explicit instructions to consider the external dimension in all sections of the IA; the clarification of which aspects of the guidelines are mandatory and which are discretionary; the allocation of resources for undertaking the IAs; the clear application of selection criteria for choosing policy proposals to undergo an extended IA; and also the thorough consultation of all interested parties including DGs and outside actors (especially NGOs)."[153]

Lussis (2004) applies a check-list model for the purpose of comparing 13 ExIAs completed between 2003 and 2004. He finds that "most of the ExIA define policy alternatives and assess them. However, there is obviously a 'methodological hole' in the areas of impact identification,

---

[153] See C. Opoku and A. Jordan, "Impact Assessment in the EU: A Global Sustainable Development Perspective", paper presented at the Berlin Conference on the Human Dimension of Global Environmental Change, 3-4 December 2004 (available at *http://www.fu-berlin.de/ffu/akumwelt/bc2004/download/opoku_jordan_f.pdf* – visited 5 December 2005).

prediction and assessment. In addition, ... most ExIAs do not bring up a clear comparison of the alternatives regarding the impact assessment."[154]

An updated scorecard of the extended impact assessments completed by the Commission as of June 2005 is illustrated in the next section, showing – if possible – even more worrying results.

2.1 How good is the Commission at impact assessment? An updated scorecard

As of June 2005, the European Commission reported to have completed 70 Extended Impact Assessments of major proposed initiatives. Fifteen ExIAs concerned proposed Directives, 14 addressed new Regulations, 22 assessed the impact of new Commission Communications and 19 ExIAs concerned the impact of proposed Commission Decisions.[155] 22 ExIAs were completed in 2003, 27 in 2004 and 22 in the first six months of 2005. The number of ExIAs completed led the Commission to highlight an increase in the coverage of impact assessment on Commission initiatives in 2004 and 2005. However, this is only partly true, as the analysis performed in this paper confirms. As a matter of fact, out of the 22 new ExIAs completed in the first six months of 2005, only 7 are true ExIAs, whereas 13 documents are short, preliminary IAs with neither quantitative nor qualitative estimates of costs and benefits. Two other documents are not qualified as ExIAs, and can be defined as background papers. As confirmed by the present analysis, the increase in the number of ExIAs is only apparent; instead, a marked decrease in the quality and comprehensiveness of assessment has occurred over time, as well as a reduced usefulness of reported results as a support for Brussels policy-makers.

---

[154] See B. Lussis, *EU Extended Impact Assessment Review*, Institut pour un Développement Durable Working Paper, 9 December 2004 (available at *http://users.skynet.be/idd/documents/EIDDD/WP01.pdf* – visited 5 December 2005).

[155] The list of ExIAs completed is available at *http://europa.eu.int/comm/ secretariat_general/impact/practice.htm* and below, in Appendix A. Of the 71 listed ExIAs, one (SEC(2004)924) is listed twice, as it served as the basis for both the Council Regulation laying down general provisions on the European Regional Development Fund, the European Social Fund and the Cohesion Fund (COM(2004)492) and for the Regulation on the European Social Fund, (COM(2004)492). As a result, the number of completed ExIAs is 70, not 71.

Such preliminary findings called for further investigation on the quality of Commission's ExIAs in the 2003-05 period. One useful and widely acknowledged way to measure the quality of performed IAs is to use a scorecard. The scorecard approach to impact assessment was successfully introduced by Robert Hahn, showing puzzling evidence on the quality of impact assessment conducted by federal agencies and the OMB in the US. In order to preserve the homogeneity of results while at the same time accounting for the EU model of impact assessment, most of the scorecard items listed by Hahn and Dudley[156] are maintained here: however, the model used for the purposes of this paper included a number of additional scorecard items, which refer to the peculiar features of the Commission's IIA model and the milestones of the Commission's Better Regulation Action plan (e.g. competitiveness, proportionality, subsidiarity, consistency with the *acquis*, use of soft law, self- and co-regulation, etc.).[157]

The next section presents the main finding of my scorecard analysis, with a caveat. Scorecards are currently subject to a heated debate in the US, as some commentators argued that such tools can hardly provide a reliable picture of the overall quality of the impact assessment exercise. Nonetheless, as recently recalled by Robert Hahn, probably the 'guru of scorecardists', the use of scorecards has proven quite useful in detecting significant flaws in the methodology used by sponsoring administrations as well as in indicating new paths for research and possible options to improve the quality of the assessment exercise.[158] In the next pages, the scorecard approach will be used for a major purpose, which is to assess whether the quality of various DGs' impact assessments supports the emphasis currently being place on the IIA model as a shortcut on the road to Lisbon.

2.1.1 Overall results of the scorecard

The results of the scorecard analysis of the first 70 ExIAs completed by Commission DGs are worrying in a number of respects. First, the problems highlighted by Lee and Kirkpatrick in their pilot study of the first 6 ExIAs completed by the Commission seem not to have been solved in subsequent

---

[156] Hahn and Dudley, op. cit.

[157] A list of scorecard items is reported in Appendix B.

[158] See R.W. Hahn, *In Defense of the Economic Analysis of Regulation*, American Enterprise Institute, Washington, D.C., 2005. Box 2 below provides a more detailed description of the debate over scorecards and CBA.

years.[159] Secondly, the end of the trial phase in 2004 has not marked any encouraging change in the quality of performed ExIAs. Thirdly, the methodology used appears far from sound, and the level of detail in the assessment is even decreasing over time. Fourthly, the presentation of results is seldom clear and almost never comprehensive, which jeopardises the usefulness of the overall analysis. Finally, some of the Commission's top priorities, such as reducing administrative burdens, ensuring consistency with the *acquis communautaire*, and exploring alternative methods of regulation, are almost never accounted for by lead DGs.

A more detailed analysis of the scorecard results reveals that:

- **Costs are seldom estimated.** Of the 70 ExIAs, only 28 (40%) quantified at least some costs and 19 (27.1%) monetised all or nearly all costs arising from the proposal. Of the latter, 13 ExIAs provided a best estimate of total costs and 9 specified a range for total cost of the proposal.

- **Costs for businesses are almost never quantified.** Only in 10 cases (14.3% of the total) were compliance costs or other costs for businesses from entry into force of a new regulation assessed. Even the impact of the proposal on EU administration costs was rarely estimated (in 16 cases or 22.9%).

- **Benefits are rarely quantified.** Although 95.7% of the ExIAs specify that the proposal will yield some benefits, 37.1% of ExIAs provide a quantification of some of the expected benefits, and in only 20 ExIAs (28.6% of the total) are some of the benefits monetised. A closer look reveals that only 10 ExIAs contain a quantification of all or nearly all benefits of the proposed initiative, a striking 14.3% of total ExIAs.

- **Specific benefits are not identified.** Out of 70 ExIAs, only 3 contain a monetisation of safety benefits, whereas the DG monetised health benefits in only 2 cases. Pollution reduction benefits were monetised in 4 cases.

- **Costs and benefits are almost never compared.** The net benefits of the proposed initiative were calculated in 12 ExIAs (17.1% of the total), only 3 of which specify a range for expected benefits. Moreover, the cost-effectiveness of the proposal was assessed in as few as 6 cases (8.6%), 5 of which include a point estimate of cost-

---

[159] See Lee and Kirkpatrick, op. cit.

effectiveness. This also implies that in 74.3% of the cases the ExIA exercise does not result in a real comparison of costs and benefits arising from the proposal.

▪ **Alternatives are seldom compared.** Most ExIAs perform an assessment of the impacts after the preferred regulatory option has been identified. As a result, even if alternative regulatory options were identified in 84.3% of ExIAs, only in 17.1% of the ExIAs were the costs of each alternative quantified, and only in 15.7% were costs monetised. Similarly, benefits were quantified only in 14.3% and monetized in 8.6% of the observed ExIAs.

▪ **The methodology used is overly simplified in most cases.** As an example, a discount rate for assessing the net present value of future costs and benefits was specified in only 2 cases (2.9% of the total). In both cases, the discount rate diverged from the 4% suggested by the Commission in its guidelines. In the report commissioned to BIPE for the ExIA of the Commission Communication on digital switchover, completed in September 2003, the chosen discount rate was 5%, whereas in the ExIA of the REACH Directive (issued in October 2003) the discount rate chosen by the lead DG was 3%.[160] Furthermore, in only one case was the value of saved life-years calculated. Finally, a sensitivity test was carried out only in 4 ExIAs (5.7%).

▪ **The presentation of results is often obscure.** Only 10 ExIAs contain an Executive Summary, and only in one case does the Executive Summary contain monetised costs, whereas in two cases it reports monetised benefits. Even if one ignores the problem of monetisation, only one ExIA includes an ES that reports non-quantified costs. Moreover, in a few cases the quality of the presentation is undoubtedly low – for example, some ExIAs are written half in English and half in French, while others don't include a table of contents or selected references.[161] The transparency and accessibility of the IA results are not facilitated by such features.

---

[160] The two ExIAs in which a discount rate was used are the Communication on the transition from analogue broadcasting to digital broadcasting: Digital switchover in Europe (SEC(2003)992) and the Framework Legislation on Chemical Substances (establishing REACH) (SEC(2003)1171).

[161] See the ExIAs on the Decision Establishing the Culture 2007 Programme (2007-2013) (SEC(2004)954) and on the Health and Consumer Protection Strategy and Programme (SEC(2005)425).

- **Environmental and social impacts are not always assessed**. Let alone the quantification of impacts, it emerges that the environmental impact of proposed regulations was considered in only 64.3% of the cases, while the social impact was accounted for in 81.4% of ExIAs.

- **Administrative burdens are not an issue in most ExIAs.** Only in 17 ExIAs (24.3%) were administrative burdens resulting from the proposal somehow assessed. This calls for further efforts in promoting the cost-awareness of administration on the burden of regulations.

- **Subsidiarity and proportionality are not always taken into due account**. Of the 70 ExIAs observed, 44 considered subsidiarity issues and 40 took into due account the principle of proportionality. This finding is in line with the Commission's statement that the proportionality principle should be further integrated in DG's *ex ante* assessments.[162]

- **Competitiveness-proofing is not performed in most ExIAs.** The goal of boosting competitiveness and achieving the Lisbon goals is becoming increasingly crucial in EU impact assessment. So far, the completed ExIAs do not appear to have taken competitiveness into due consideration. Only 15 extended assessments (21.4%) carry some form of competitiveness-proofing.

- **Soft law, self- and co-regulation are rarely included in alternative options.** In spite of the Commission's increased focus on 'de-ossifying' EU regulation, as few as 8 ExIAs consider some form of soft law amongst the alternative options. Likewise, in 6 cases the lead DG considered co-regulation and in 5 cases self-regulation was considered to be a possible alternative, whether or not such option was eventually endorsed.

- **Not all DGs are created equal.** There seems to be *prima facie* evidence that some of the DGs that led the impact assessment process are better equipped than others for undertaking such task. Examples of DGs that have performed their tasks rather well are DG Information Society, DG Enterprise, DG Research, DG Sanco, DG Education and Culture and DG Agriculture, with mixed results for DG Environment, DG Energy and Transport and DG Internal Market.

---

[162] See European Commission Staff Working Paper, *Impact Assessment: Next Steps*, op. cit. For a better definition of proportionality, see section 3.2 below.

Other DGs – such as JAI, JLS, REGIO and TAXUD – seem to lag behind in terms of expertise in carrying out a complete evaluation.

- **The timing of consultation can be improved**. The good news is that almost all ExIAs (94.3%) report some form of consultation. However, in some cases consultation took place when the Commission had already identified the relevant option, and did not lead to major changes. Only in roughly half of the ExIAs did the results of the consultation seem to have contributed to the choice of the regulatory option and/or to major changes in the crafting of the final proposal.

In summary, there seems to be a stark contrast between the Commission's increased emphasis on impact assessment and the quality of assessments performed so far by Commission DGs. The grey picture gets even darker, in many respects, if one observes the scorecard for ExIAs in its evolution over time.

2.1.2 Has the quality of ExIAs increased over time?

When the IIA was introduced, the Commission specified that the procedure would be subject to a trial period until the end of 2004, and that it expected ExIAs to be less comprehensive and complete during the trial period. Accordingly, one would expect to observe an increased quality of ExIAs over time. The scorecard analysis performed in the present work, however, suggests that things went differently.

Figure 5 shows the results of the analysis for the major scorecard items related to cost assessment. As clearly emerges from the figure, the percentage of ExIAs in which the lead DG has quantified/monetised costs decreased from 42.9% in 2003 to 36.4% in 2005. But the percentage of ExIAs that actually monetised all or nearly all costs was much smaller, accounting for 28.6% in 2003, to 33.3% in 2004 and as low as 18.6% in 2005. Accordingly, the share of ExIAs that provided either a best estimate or a range for total costs climbed from 33.3% to 37% from 2003 to 2004, but then fell to 22.7% in 2005.

Similar results emerge from the analysis of data on benefit assessment. As reported in Figure 6, while in 2003, 57.1% of ExIAs quantified at least some of the benefits arising from the proposed initiative, the percentage fell to 33.3% in 2004 and to 22.7% in 2005. Similarly, the percentage of ExIAs that monetised at least some of the expected benefits fell from 47.6% in 2005 to 18.2% in 2005. Interestingly, only one ExIA monetised all or nearly all benefits in 2005.

Figure 5. Quality of ExIAs in 2003, 2004 and 2005: Selected scorecard items on cost assessment

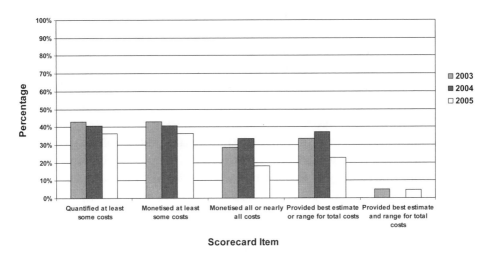

Figure 6. Quality of ExIAs in 2003, 2004 and 2005: Selected scorecard items on benefit assessment

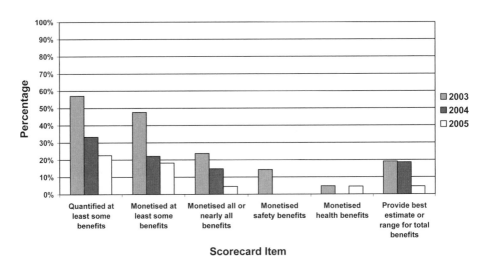

Moreover, very few ExIAs took account of health and safety benefits of the proposals, even though many assessed proposals had some form of environmental or health-related impact. Finally, not more than 19% of ExIAs calculated either a best estimate or a range for total benefits in 2003, but this percentage fell dramatically in 2005, with only one ExIA carrying such a useful calculation.

Moreover, Figure 7 shows similar decreases in the accuracy of estimates as regards four scorecard items related to overall impact assessment and analysis of alternative policy options. Here again, the percentage of ExIAs in which the lead DG calculated either the net benefits or the cost-effectiveness of the chosen option decreased from 28.6% in 2003 and 33.3% in 2004 to 9.1% in 2005. Similarly, in the first six months of 2005, only 4.5% of ExIAs compared the cost of selected alternative policy options in quantitative terms, and no ExIA carried a quantitative comparison of the benefits of selected alternative options in the same period. On the contrary, such a quantitative exercise was carried out in 23.8% (costs) and 33.3% (benefits) of ExIAs in 2003, and in 22.2% (costs) and 11.1% (benefits) of ExIAs in 2004. As a result, if in 2003 lead DGs calculated either the net benefits or the cost-effectiveness of alternatives for 28.6% of the proposals subject to ExIAs, in 2004 the corresponding figure fell to 22.2% and in the first semester of 2005 – interestingly enough – no ExIA carried an assessment of net benefits or cost-effectiveness of alternative regulatory options whatsoever.

Figure 7. Quality of ExIAs in 2003, 2004 and 2005: Selected items on overall impact assessment

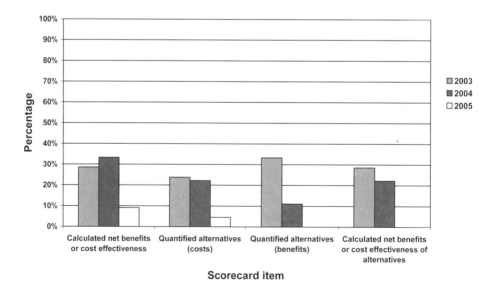

Finally, it is useful to assess whether the ExIAs performed by the Commission's DGs in 2003-05 adequately mirror the peculiar features of the IIA model as well as the top priorities indicated by the Commission for boosting competitiveness and sustainable development through the quality of EU legislation. Figure 8, thus, compares the ExIAs performed by Commission DGs in 2003-05 by reporting the percentage of assessments that carried some mention of the environmental and the social impact of the proposal, as well as the principles of competitiveness, subsidiarity and proportionality.

Figure 8. Quality of ExIAs in 2003, 2004 and 2005: Selected items on comprehensiveness of assessment

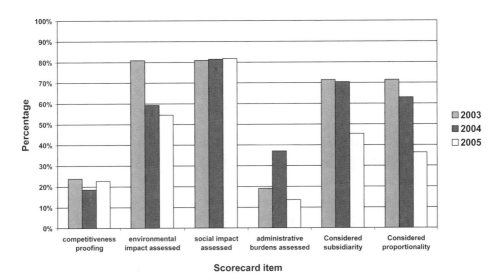

As emerges from Figure 8, the consistency of the proposal with the goal of competitiveness was tackled only in a few cases in the whole period observed, more precisely in 23.8% of ExIAs in 2003, in 18.5% in 2004 and in 22.7% of the 2005 assessments. And, while social implications of the proposed initiatives were assessed in roughly 80% of all ExIAs in all the three years observed, environmental issues have been gradually discarded by lead DGs, falling from 81% of all ExIAs in 2003, to 59.3% in 2004 and 54.5% in 2005. Finally, subsidiarity and proportionality were accounted for in most of ExIAs in 2003 and 2004, but were addressed in only 45.5% (subsidiarity) and 36.4% (proportionality) of the cases in the ExIAs completed in the first six months of 2005.

In summary, and interestingly enough, evidence reveals that the quality of Extended Impact Assessments performed by the Commission during the first years of implementation of the new IIA model has been constantly and remarkably declining. At first blush, it would seem at least hazardous to detect, in the performed assessments, the virtuous potential that would transform *ex ante* impact assessment into that powerful tool that the EU would need to reach Lisbon on the wings of better regulation. Put differently, the current implementation of the IIA model seems hardly geared towards contributing to the efficiency, effectiveness and overall quality of EU legislation.

Efforts towards improving the current IIA model, with specific emphasis on its procedural dimension, have been recently undertaken both by the European Parliament and the Council. Moreover, the Commission itself seems to have realised that the results of the first experimental phase are more disappointing than they *prima facie* appear, and issued a new Communication on better regulation and impact assessment as well as new guidelines on how to carry out a methodologically sound IA in the first six months of 2005. Sections 2.2 and 2.3 describe the proposals put forward by other EU institutions and the new Commission Communication, respectively. Chapter 3 explores possible ways in which the current implementation of the IIA model can be improved by the Commission over the next few years.

2.2 Strengthening inter-institutional dialogue: Towards a new European Impact Assessment?

As recalled earlier in this report, in the immediate aftermath of the Commission White Paper on European Governance, the European Parliament complained about the lack of inter-institutional cooperation between the Commission and other EU institutions on the issue of better regulation and in particular impact assessment.[163] After the Council meetings held in Seville in 21-22 June 2002 and in Brussels on 20-21 March 2003, the Commission, the Parliament and the Council decided to undertake a number of joint initiatives to improve the quality of law-making at EU and member state level, and issued an Inter-institutional Agreement on better law-making which also covers the issue of impact assessment as a tool to improve the quality of legislation.[164] The Agreement

---

[163] See notes 145-146 and accompanying text.

[164] OJ 2003/C 321/01, 23 December 2003.

clearly states that a more frequent use of impact assessments (both *ex ante* and *ex post*) will help ensure that EU legislation is of good quality, meaning that it is "clear, simple and effective".[165] The Agreement also specifies that the Commission will continue to take the lead on the development of the integrated impact assessment model, and the results will have to be made fully available to the Parliament, the Council and the general public. It also points out that whenever the co-decision procedure applies, the Parliament and the Council "may, on the basis of jointly defined criteria and procedures, have impact assessments carried out prior to the adoption of any substantive amendment, either at first reading or at the conciliation stage". In view of such an overlap of impact assessment procedures, the three institutions agreed to carry out an assessment of their respective experiences and to consider the "possibility of establishing a common methodology".[166]

The Interinstitutional Agreement, however, was followed by a number of stand-alone initiatives by the three institutions. The Parliament was particularly active in the monitoring and evaluation of the currently enacted impact assessment model. Of particular interest is the so-called 'Doorn motion' – from the name of Rapporteur Bert Doorn – that resulted in the Parliament Resolution on the "Assessment of the impact of Community legislation and the consultation procedure".[167] The Doorn motion proposes substantial changes in the Commission's impact assessment model, in view of the creation of what is defined as a European Impact Assessment (EIA) procedure. The main features of the EIA are as follows:

- The Commission, the Parliament and the Council adopt the *same standards* for impact assessment.

- Any proposal by the Commission will be subjected to a *global cost estimate*.

- The global cost estimate is performed by the official responsible *in consultation with an audit* reporting directly to the President of the Commission, which is also in charge of monitoring the cost estimate.

---

[165] Ibid., §25.

[166] Ibid., §30.

[167] Parliament Resolution 2004/A5-0221, 24 March 2004.

- The Parliament and the Council accept from the Commission only proposals accompanied by a *cost estimate* and an *impact assessment*.

- The Commission, the Council and the Parliament must lay down a *cost threshold* above which an Extended IA must be carried out.

- Not only the Commission proposal, but *also all amendments* by the Parliament and the Council that exceed the cost threshold *must undergo an extended impact assessment*.

- In order to implement such a new procedure: a) the *Parliament will set up an audit* "with whatever reasonable means [it] has at its disposal"; and b) the *Council will set up an audit* in the Council Secretariat.

Thus, the Doorn motion calls for the establishment of a common procedure in which three parallel audits are created for the joint implementation of the European Impact Assessment model by the three institutions, following commonly agreed criteria. No doubt, the implementation of such procedure would entail a major departure from the Commission's integrated impact assessment model as set out in 2002. And it is hardly questionable that the implementation of the new EIA procedure would create the world's most complex and sophisticated model of *ex ante* evaluation of proposed regulations. The EIA would at once present an unmatched comprehensiveness, incorporating the assessment of the economic, social and environmental impact of proposed regulations and proposed amendments, and a three-tiered audit system with enhanced inter-institutional competition. *Prima facie,* the model would also draw valuable lessons from the US and the UK experience – most notably, the introduction of a cost threshold for extended impact assessment and the appointment of *ad hoc* independent audits reporting directly to the General Secretariat of the Commission, the Parliament and the Council Secretariat. Finally, the proposed EIA model would encourage the submission of far-reaching amendments to Commission proposals, thus strengthening the collaborative dimension of Community legislation.

However, the Doorn model also elicits substantial concerns. First, the proposed EIA model does not seem to provide an encouraging contribution to the goal of cutting red tape and reducing administration costs. The proposed procedure is likely to appear at least cumbersome and risks substantially slowing down the approval of new regulations. Secondly, the administrative burden of the proposed EIA model is likely to be quite heavy: the procedure actually adds at least one procedural step (the initial cost assessment) plus all cost assessments, preliminary impact assessment and extended impact assessments that have to be carried out by the proponent institution in case of major amendments. Thirdly, the EIA model would be significantly more costly than the (already quite burdensome) IIA model adopted by the Commission. At a minimum, three new, dedicated structures (the audits) would have to be created, and in some cases external expertise would be required in order to complete the Extended Impact Assessment of proposals exceeding the cost threshold, Fourthly, the cost-savings potential of the proposed cost threshold is at least uncertain, given that the Commission's IIA model already mandates ExIAs for a selected number of major proposals to be identified in the Annual Policy Strategy decision in February each year. Fifthly, transaction costs are likely to increase, leaving room also for strategic behaviour by each of the three institutions vis-à-vis the others. And finally, the decision about the cost threshold and the common standards to be adopted for the performance of extended impact assessments would prove absolutely delicate and crucial for the efficiency and effectiveness of the new model.

In summary, the Doorn motion for a European Impact Assessment seems overly ambitious and hard to implement at EU (and at any other) level. The Parliament resolution was adopted a few months before the Commission issued its first Progress Report on the implementation of its IIA model, highlighting that the procedure is already quite costly and burdensome for responsible officials. Thence, to set up such a complex system without facing more inefficiency would be almost impossible. As will be clarified in the next sections, an impact assessment of the impact assessment procedure (a meta-IA) would certainly help in defining the most efficient model to be adopted. Against this backdrop, what is clear from the Doorn motion is that the Parliament does not consider the current IIA model to be fully satisfactory, with specific respect to the Parliament's right to propose far-reaching amendments and command its own impact assessments on the Commission's proposed new regulations.

Faced with such an institutional tension, the Council has adopted a milder position on the prospects of EU impact assessment. But activities at the Council have increased after the Finance Ministers of Ireland, the Netherlands, Luxembourg and the UK launched the so-called 'four presidencies' initiative for a joint action on regulatory reform on 26 January 2004.[168] The four presidencies' letter suggests that the selection of proposals

---

[168] The joint statement is available at *http://www.hm-treasury.gov.uk/media/47C54/ jirf_0104.pdf* – last visited 7 December 2005.

to be subjected to ExIAs should be agreed with the Council annually, before the APS (Annual Policy Strategy) decision by the Commission. Furthermore, the presidencies stated the need for more formal quality control on the Commission's ExIAs before the publication of the proposal. But the letter also called for competitiveness-proofing of all proposed regulations by the Competitiveness Council, therefore advocating greater involvement of the Council in the procedure. Finally, the four presidencies called for greater use of review clauses in EU legislation and for a greater use of "imaginative, outcome-based" approaches to regulation, such as the New Approach based on essential requirements and mutual recognition.[169]

Further emphasis on strengthening the competitiveness dimension of impact assessment performed by the Commission came from the Competitiveness Council in its meetings held in May and November 2004.[170] The Council also announced a pilot project aimed at carrying out impact assessments on proposed Council amendments, to be evaluated in May 2005. The Council's increased involvement in the matter of better regulation culminated in the specification of a list of 15 priorities for simplification of EU legislation in November 2004, which included intervention aimed at streamlining regulation in a number of sectors.[171] Finally, a joint letter of the Irish, Dutch, Luxembourg, UK, Austrian and Finnish Presidencies of the EU emphasised the need to tackle the issue of administrative costs of existing and prospective regulation, as well as the need to strengthen the competitiveness dimension and the Council involvement in the Commission's IIA model.[172] Further pressure on the Commission to progress in the implementation of the integrated impact assessment model as a competitiveness-oriented policy tool was exerted

---

[169] For information on the New Approach, see *http://europa.eu.int/comm/enterprise/newapproach/index_en.htm* – visited 5 December 2005.

[170] See the Press Release of the 2583rd Meeting of the Council, held in Brussels, on 17-18 May 2004, in which the Council committed to "contribute to enhancing the competitiveness dimension of the integrated impact assessment process, on the basis of inputs from Member States".

[171] See the Note from the Council Meeting held in Brussels on 23 November 2005 (available at *http://www.smallbusinesseurope.org/Issues/Better%20Regulation/1101396743/Comp_Concl* – visited 5 December 2005).

[172] See "Advancing Regulatory Reform in Europe", a Joint Statement of the Irish, Dutch, Luxembourg, UK, Austrian and Finnish Presidencies of the European Union, 7 December 2004 (available at *http://www.hm-treasury.gov.uk/media/95A/52/6presidencies.pdf* – last visited 7 December 2005).

until the European Council meeting held on 22-23 March 2005, where the Commission presented its new Communication on Better Regulation for Growth and Jobs in the European Union of 16 March 2005.[173]

2.3 The 2005 Communication on impact assessment and the June 2005 Guidelines: Back to basics?

The Commission assessed the first results of its new Integrated Impact Assessment model in December 2004, which drew a mixed picture of the progress made in improving the quality of EU legislation. A first measure was to request services to establish 'Roadmaps' for the initiatives they have put forward for inclusion in the Annual Policy Strategy and in the Commission's Work Programme.[174] But several other sources of pressure were calling for major efforts from the Commission to significantly increase the momentum of better regulation, with specific emphasis on strengthening and improving impact assessment methods. First, as explained in the previous section, the Parliament and the Council urged the Commission to accept a greater involvement of all EU institutions in the procedure, by extending impact assessment to major amendments and defining common methodologies for carrying out assessments in all three institutions. Secondly, the worrying signals of delay shown by the mid-term review of the Lisbon strategy in February 2005, called for greater emphasis on fostering employment and growth and reducing the administrative burdens of regulation, shifting the focus from sustainable development to competitiveness, and from integrated impact assessment to economic assessment, sometimes focusing exclusively on business compliance costs.[175] Thirdly, the failure to reach the goal of achieving a 25% reduction in the volume of the *acquis communautaire* by 2005, stated by the Prodi Commission, suggested the need for new efforts in the field of simplification. Finally, the decision to extend the impact assessment

---

[173] COM(2005)97, 16 March 2005.

[174] See note 147 and accompanying text.

[175] In its Communication to the Spring European Council on "Working together for Growth and Jobs – A New Start for the Lisbon Strategy", COM(2005)24 of 2 February 2005, the Commission suggested that "[a] new approach to regulation should seek to remove burdens and cut red tape unnecessary for reaching the underlying policy objectives. Better Regulation should be a cornerstone for decision making at all levels of the Union."

procedure to all the initiatives included in the Commission's 2005 Legislative and Work Programme (roughly 100) contrasted starkly with evidence that the scheduled IAs had not been completed and had exhibited significant methodological problems, calling for a refinement of the guidelines and a redress of the proportionality principle.

The Commission took action in March 2005, with a new Communication on Better Regulation for Growth and Jobs in the European Union, defining the achievements of the early years of implementation of the IIA as "first steps in what must be a permanent effort".[176] The Communication lays down important changes in the IIA procedure and re-launches the role of impact assessment as part of the Lisbon strategy. The Communication's vibrant statement on the need to boost better regulation initiatives at all levels resulted in the launch of three key actions, to be reviewed in 2007, devoted to: i) the design and application of better regulation tools at EU level; ii) a closer collaboration with member states to ensure a consistent application of better regulation principles; and iii) a stronger, constructive dialogue with all EU regulators, member states and other stakeholders.

The main features of the Commission's new strategy on better regulation and impact assessment can be summarised as follows:

▪ Although the IIA is rooted in the sustainable development principle and its integrated nature is not under discussion, there is an *urge to strengthen the assessment of the economic impact* of proposed regulations – compared to the social and environmental impact assessments – in view of the increased importance of the competitiveness principle.

▪ The Commission plans to develop a methodology to better integrate the *measurement of administrative costs* in its IIA model, and has launched a pilot project for the quantification of such burdens that will produce the first results in late 2005, together with a trial new methodology called the 'EU net administrative cost model'.[177]

---

[176] See Communication on Better Regulation for Growth and Jobs in the European Union, op. cit.

[177] See Commission Staff Working Paper, Annex to the 2005 Communication on Better Regulation for Growth and Jobs in the European Union, *Minimising Administrative Costs Imposed by Legislation, Detailed Outline of a Possible EU Net Administrative Cost Model*, SEC(2005)175, 16 March 2005. Recall, in addition, that the UK Presidency stated its intention to develop a common methodology on

- The Commission will reinforce the external validation of the methodology adopted for the IIA, and plans to have a "comprehensive independent *evaluation of the Impact Assessment system* as it has evolved and been implemented since 2002", scheduled for early 2006.[178]

- The IIA model will be extended to the Parliament and the Council, where the co-decision procedure applies, *for all major amendments* to Commission proposals.

- The Commission is strengthening its efforts on streamlining and simplifying the existing regulatory *corpus* by *screening pending legislative proposals* that have remained idle for a significant period of time and that have not been subjected to impact assessment or whose IA revealed major weaknesses. A subsequent Communication, issued in September 2005, withdrew 56 pending proposals dated before 1 January 2004 and 12 proposals presented in 2004.[179]

- Moreover, the Commission launched a three-year *action plan for simplification*, which aims to repeal, codify, recast or modify 222 basic legislations and over 1,400 related legal acts in the next three years. The action plan – contained in a Communication issued on October 25, 2005, initially focuses on heavily regulated sectors, such as cars, waste and construction, and will then address simplification in other sectors such as foodstuffs, cosmetics, pharmaceuticals or services will follow.[180]

---

measuring administrative burdens, based on the Standard Cost Model successfully applied in the Netherlands.

[178] p. 6 (emphasis in original).

[179] See the Commission Communication, COM(2005)462 (Outcome of the screening of legislative proposals pending before the legislator). The withdrawn proposals were related to sectors such as agriculture, competition policy, development, economic and financial affairs, enlargement, enterprise and industry, environment, fisheries and maritime affairs, internal market and services, justice, freedom and security, external relations, research, health and consumer protection, codification, taxation and customs unions, trade, energy and transport.

[180] See the Commission Communication, COM(2005)535, Implementing the Community Lisbon programme: A strategy for the simplification of the regulatory environment.

- The Commission will create two networks of experts. A first network will group high-level national regulatory experts for the development of a "coherent set of common indicators to monitor progress as regards the quality of the regulatory environment" both at EU and member state level. Another network will be composed of experts in better regulation issues, including academicians and practitioners from the economic, social and environmental fields, who will be called to advise the Commission on a case-by-case basis as regards the methodology adopted for carrying out the IIA.

To those who have followed the debate on the implementation of the Commission's IIA model since 2003, these changes came as no surprise. And those who have seen substantial continuity between the Communication issued in 2002 and the new strategy laid out by the Commission should not overlook the remarkable deviation made by the Commission in targeting its IIA model. The IIA is coming back to the somewhat tight walls of cost-benefit analysis, compliance cost assessment and simplification initiatives. This might seem as a thorough reconsideration of the overly ambitious initial goal of establishing a comprehensive, burdensome IA procedure without taking into account the existing legislative *acquis*, without relying on external expertise and without involving other EU institutions. The Commission has now taken a step backwards from such a challenging endeavour, with the stated aim of getting to grips with a more reliable, focused procedure whose main purpose is to help the EU and member states to reach a level-playing field on the road to Lisbon. Also the greater attention to *ex post* monitoring and the plan to have a meta-IA to be conducted in early 2006 substantiate this impression.

The 'back-to-basics' hypothesis is supported by the new Guidelines issued by the Commission in June 2005.[181] The Technical Annex to the Guidelines devotes special attention to methods for assessing the economic impact of proposed regulations, in particular the impact on growth, competitiveness and employment. A specific section is also dedicated to the assessment of administrative costs imposed by legislation.[182]

---

[181] See European Commission, Impact Assessment Guidelines, SEC(2005)971, 15 June 2005.

[182] The Guidelines anticipate that in early 2006 an internet-based software will be introduced in all DGs to help officials in the drafting of IA forms, in the problem

In summary, the first years of the Commission's IIA model introduced in 2002 have attracted growing attention to impact assessment as a tool to improve the quality of EU legislation. It is far from being a panacea, however. Impact assessment has proven – in some international experiences – to provide valuable assistance at the early stage of policy formulation, and, as such, ranks amongst the key drivers of the now re-targeted Lisbon strategy. However, the Commission has undertaken a 'trial and error' phase which has ultimately resulted in a step backwards, towards a more 'canonic' model of regulatory impact assessment, which will arguably be made more effective by an increased emphasis on administrative costs, compliance costs and cost-benefit analysis. This seems *prima facie* to achieve the valuable result of bringing the Commission's initial endeavour 'back to Earth', in line with the widely acknowledged 'think-real' approach.

In the years to come, most of the newly stated objectives will have to pass scrutiny as drivers of enhanced legislative quality, greater inter-institutional dialogue and increased administrative efficiency. Chapter 3 offers some possible options to get the EU Better Regulation Action Plan back on the Lisbon track and to achieve a more satisfactory model of policy evaluation at EU and member state level.

---

definition and in the identification of potential economic, social and environmental impacts. Ibid., section 4.2., p. 26.

3. Can the IIA be improved? Roadmaps for the Years Ahead

As recalled in the previous chapter, while reviewing its overall strategy for better regulation and impact assessment, the Commission stated that the improvements already achieved in the impact assessment procedure – which the Commission considers to be significant – are only to be considered as 'a first step' in what should be a permanent effort towards better policy-making at EU and member state level. Next steps already scheduled by the Commission include the new Communication on the simplification of EU legislation issued in October 2005 and the comprehensive independent evaluation of the IIA model to be launched in early 2006.[183]

In this section, possible improvements to the current model are analysed under a more theoretical perspective and presented in the form of 'roadmaps'. Possible amendments include the following:

- The IIA should be based on an *improved and standardised methodology*, in order to become a reliable and effective aid to policy-making. The current scorecard of the Commission's Extended Impact Assessments shows quite disappointing results, as found by the few studies undertaken in this field and confirmed by the scorecard illustrated in section 2.1. In addition, in the future EU officials will have to reconcile the narrow focus of the emerging 'EU net administrative cost model' with the substantially broader scope of the Integrated Impact Assessment model – a further source of complexity for already challenged administrations.

---

[183] For a list of evaluation initiatives currently underway at the Commission, see Annex II of the *Annual Evaluation Review 2004 – Overview of the Commission's Findings and Activities*, SEC(2005)587, May 2005.

- The impact assessment model can be made more *'proportionate'* and *'flexible'*: the depth and scope of the assessment, as well as the variables and options that regulators must take into account while carrying out an *ex ante* regulatory impact assessment should vary depending upon the expected impact of the proposed regulation as well as whether the proposed regulation will allegedly have an impact on the Commission's regulatory agenda and/or major regulatory principles (as happens in the UK experience). Accordingly, administrations might choose different methodologies depending on the expected impact of the proposed initiative (e.g. adopting cost-effectiveness analysis instead of full cost-benefit analysis, thereby reducing the administrative burden).[184]

- The IIA model can be made *'sector-specific'*, meaning that different theoretical frameworks can be developed for *ex ante* impact assessments in some key sectors of the European economy (for instance, high-tech industries, financial markets, services of general interest, etc.). Sector-specificity of impact assessment procedures might also incorporate the proportionality principle, avoiding redundancies in the procedure and, consequently, increasing efficiency.

- The IIA model can be made more *'internally consistent'* and *'cost-effective'*. For this purpose, there is a strong urge to further analyse the organisational dimension of the EU model, applying an organisation-theoretic and a game-theoretic approach in order to suggest possible amendments to the EU model: this would help to reduce cost duplications, facilitate institutional accountability, involve all stakeholders in important proposed regulations and speed up the RIA procedure.

- The EU impact assessment procedure can be made more *'transparent'*. Consultation procedures and public consultations are still under

---

[184] In its IA guidelines, the Commission recalls that administrations should "[a]dapt the level of analysis to the likely impact of the initiative being examined (principle of proportionate analysis). In other words, the amount of work and the depth of the analysis for the impact assessment should be balanced against the significance of the proposal concerned." See the Commission's Impact Assessment Guidelines, op. cit., p. 9. As will be recalled in section 3.2, the idea of 'getting things in proportion' has probably permeated the impact assessment model more deeply in Denmark than in any other member state.

development in the new EU model. More in detail, it is still unclear whether the current model allows for sufficient transparency and, at the same time, shields EU administrations from the risk of being captured by powerful interest groups.

- The procedure should take into account the organisational changes needed within EU administrations as a consequence of the introduction of the new model. In particular, the implementation of the new model must be mirrored and enabled by a corresponding *cultural change* in administrations, which goes beyond the mere capability to 'think outside the box', implying stronger accountability and performance-oriented behaviour, in line with the main lessons drawn from New Public Management as implemented in the UK and in a number of other OECD countries.

- Setting up an efficient and effective procedure for *ex ante* evaluation is doomed to remain an incomplete measure, if methods for *ex post evaluation and monitoring* are not correspondingly fine-tuned. Current methods of *ex post* evaluation available at the European Commission appear insufficient for this purpose, whereas in the US the publication of yearly reports on the costs and benefits of major regulations has become a reality. Europe, in this respect, needs its own 'grand experiment'.

- The impact assessment model adopted in the EU should be made more attuned to the concept of subsidiarity by introducing measures to provide for *a gradual convergence of RIA models implemented at member state (central and local government) level*. This implies a stronger coordination/convergence between impact assessment procedures adopted by EU member states – an issue that has gained even stronger momentum following the May 2004 enlargement – which require accession countries to quickly adopt the *acquis communautaire* and establish new procedures aimed at ensuring the quality of regulations as well as their compatibility with the peculiar regulatory context of individual countries in transition.[185]

---

[185] A similar concern is expressed by the "Joint Initiative on Regulatory Reform" undertaken by the Finance Ministers of Ireland, the Netherlands, Luxembourg and the UK on 26 January 2004. The statement clearly indicates that "improved regulatory processes and structures at Member State level will also make an important contribution to the economic performance of the Union and the realisation of competitive benefits from the internal market. Member States should

- The Commission should *issue guidelines to ensure the competitiveness of new and existing regulations*. This effort can be modelled on the corresponding endeavour undertaken in the US in 1986 with the creation of the Council on Competitiveness, whose mandate was to review and – where appropriate – suggest the elimination of any US regulation that could exert a negative impact on US competitiveness. The EU Competitiveness Council could take on such a demanding task to a greater extent than it has done so far.

- An *ad hoc oversight agency* for better regulation should be created, in line with international best practices. The main functions of such a new agency would include advocacy, consulting, oversight, challenge, coordination, reporting and institutional relations.

The following sections are dedicated to a more detailed explanation of these possible amendments to the IIA model.

3.1   Roadmap 1 – Improving methodology and introducing cost-benefit analysis

As explained in section 2.1 above, the Commission's implementation of the IIA model has been characterised by significant methodological flaws, which are only partially justified by the experimental nature of the exercises undertaken. An improvement in the soundness of the methodology adopted by lead DGs in performing ExIAs is certainly a necessary condition for improving the effectiveness of impact assessment as a better regulation tool in the EU. Accordingly, this section puts forward some suggestions for improving the methodological soundness of ExIAs without unduly raising its impact on DGs' budgets.

One straightforward critique of the implementation of the IIA model comes from the almost complete lack of quantitative analyses, most notably

---

commit to ongoing national regulatory reform initiatives, including the introduction of effective systems of impact assessment for new legislation and simplification programmes, building on the best practice that can be shared across Member States". The statement was then welcomed at the March 2004 European Council, which called upon the Commission and the Council to pursue a number of actions to drive forward the reform programme. At the end of the Dutch Presidency, the initiative was extended to the forthcoming Austrian and Finnish Presidencies. See the Joint Statement on "Advancing Regulatory Reform in Europe", issued 7 December 2004.

of cost-benefit analysis (CBA), normally considered as the most reliable, useful and comprehensive way to provide regulators with a litmus test for identifying regulatory options worth being undertaken. The reliability of CBA as a neutral tool for policy-makers has been constantly under debate in economic theory, and its wide application in the US – where the goal of creating a cost-benefit State has been often evoked – has been recently the subject of fierce debate.[186]

Box 2 summarises the main arguments in favour and against CBA as outlined in the current US debate. What emerges is the finding that CBA is useful only if regulators understand its potential as well as its limits. Accordingly, CBA should be considered as a proxy for comparing alternative regulatory options, rather than a crystal ball enabling policy-makers to foresee the exact impact of yet-to-be-introduced regulations, and as such should be used only when its impact on alternative options is neutral – e.g. when costs and benefits of alternative policy options are expressed in the same measurement unit and occur over a similar time span.

As a matter of fact, improving the methodology does not necessarily mean that all ExIAs should contain a complete monetisation and comparison of prospective direct and indirect costs and benefits. In many cases, a full-fledged cost-benefit analysis is too costly an exercise compared to the expected impact of the proposal to be assessed. Economists normally consider cost-effectiveness analysis (CEA) to be a viable alternative in such cases, and even wholly qualitative analysis can provide valuable support to the policy-maker, provided that it is performed with scientific accuracy.[187]

With this *caveat* in mind, a first suggestion to improve the methodology used by DGs is to *mandate CBA at least for major regulations*, whose impact justifies the cost of such an exercise, *and more generally promote the use of quantitative analysis* (e.g. CBA, CEA, Risk-Risk analysis,

---

[186] On cost-benefit analysis, see M.D. Adler and E.A. Posner, *Cost-Benefit Analysis: Legal, Economic, and Philosophical Perspectives*, Chicago, IL: University of Chicago Press, 2001; A.E. Boardman, *Cost-benefit Analysis: Concepts and Practice*, Upper Saddle River, NJ: Prentice Hall, 1997; and M. Munger, *Analyzing Policy: Choices, Conflicts and Practices*, New York, NY: W.W. Norton & Co., 2000.

[187] The next section (Roadmap 2) will deal with the issue of proportionality more extensively. For insightful suggestions on how to use qualitative and quantitative estimates, see K. Arrow, et al., *Benefit-Cost Analysis in Environmental, Health, and Safety Regulation: A Statement of Principles*, AEI-Brookings Joint Center for Regulatory Studies, Washington, D.C., 1996.

economic modelling, etc.) whenever feasible. In this respect, Robert Hahn and Robert Litan have recently recommended that the Commission should issue a Communication specifying that the primary objective of regulation is to maximise net benefits.[188]

Box 2. The debate on CBA in the US

Over the past few years, the reliability of quantitative CBA in regulatory impact assessment has been the subject of heated debate amongst economists and practitioners, especially in the US. Following the path-breaking work of Robert Hahn of the AEI-Brookings Joint Center for Regulatory Studies and Frank Morrall of the OMB in the US, some authors have started criticising the use of CBA by defining it as a non-neutral, anti-regulatory tool that provides a misguided view of the costs and benefits of regulations. According to authors such as Ackerman, Heinzerling and Massey, the application of CBA to a number of past decisions would have had disastrous consequence in terms of efficiency and public health.[189] The authors mention three case studies: the removal of lead from gasoline in the 1970s and 1980s, the decision *not* to dam the Grand Canyon for hydroelectric power in the 1960s and the strict regulation of workplace exposure to vinyl chloride in 1974. They argue that use of cost-benefit analysis "would have gotten the answer wrong in all three cases"; thus, they conclude that CBA should not play a central role, at least for regulations involving substantial health, environmental or safety issues. CBA, according to Ackerman and Massey, amounts to "knowing the price of everything and the value of nothing". In particular, the benefits of environmentally sensible regulations are often priceless, and unlikely to be captured by CBA, "an opaque and technically intricate process accessible only to experts, and one that all too frequently recommends rejection of sensible policies, on the grounds that their costs exceed economists' estimates of their benefits."[190]

Other authors, such as Richard Parker and David Driesen have heavily criticised the neutrality of CBA and shaped it as an anti-regulatory instrument for policy-making. Parker also argued that Hahn's scorecard analysis is biased

---

[188] See Hahn and Litan, op. cit., p. 500. Needless to say, following this suggestion would prove, at least to a certain extent, inconsistent with the current shift away from net benefits, and towards the minimization of administrative costs in the EU.

[189] See F. Ackerman, L. Heinzerling and R. Massey, *Applying Cost-Benefit to Past Decisions: Was environmental protection ever a good idea?*, Georgetown Public Law Research Paper No. 576161, Georgetown University, August 2004.

[190] See F. Ackerman and L. Heinzerling, *Priceless: On Knowing the Price of Everything and the Value of Nothing*, New York, NY: The New Press, 2004.

since it encompasses all rules for which a RIA was required – but RIA is required for the costliest rules, not for the most beneficial ones.[191] Similarly, Driesen finds that the non-neutrality of CBA is *in re ipsa*, since postulating that regulatory costs should not exceed benefits will never lead to promoting greater protection of health, safety or the environment. He also argues that "[a]ssigning monetary values to avoided illness, death, and environmental damage raises ethical questions and serious technical problems. Monetisation requires very controversial value assumptions and in many cases proves impossible. The typical outcome of CBA includes a dollar value for expected costs and a wide range of dollar values for a few quantifiable benefits. This range often proves so large that it deprives CBA of any capacity it might have to objectively guide decision-making ... many important environmental, health, and safety effects cannot be quantified at all."[192]

Another critique to CBA was the indeterminacy of the approach to be adopted in comparing costs and benefits. Although the OMB has always specified that it uses CBA by specifying that regulatory costs cannot exceed benefits, approaches to CBA can vary, highlighting the non-neutral value judgments that underline benefit-cost tests as a policy-making tool. CBA approaches have been divided as follows:

- An *indeterminate position*, which takes CBA as one of a number of available tools to inspire legislative decisions, representing economic efficiency as one possible policy objective together with ethical, safety, environmental, social and other issues. If this is the case, a full estimation of all expected benefits and costs is often too costly and time-consuming, and might delay enforcement.[193]

- A *benefits cannot outweigh costs* approach, currently adopted at the OMB, but seen as "inherently not neutral" since "[i]f cost falls below benefit, this criterion does not require a more stringent standard. But if cost outweighs benefit, agencies are forced to weaken their standard in order to comply."[194]

- A *cost equals benefits* or *'optimizing benefits'* approach, which entails that regulatory interventions are planned only when they prove inherently efficient, i.e. up to a level where the marginal benefit of the intervention equals the marginal cost. This is certainly the more neutral version of CBA, but it is probably difficult to implement and is not adopted by the OMB.

---

[191] See R. Parker, "Grading the Government", *University of Chicago Law Review*, 70: 1346, October 2003.

[192] See David Driesen's White Paper, *Is Cost-Benefit Analysis Neutral?*, 2 February 2005 (available at *http://ssrn.com/abstract=663602* – visited 5 December 2005), p. 7.

[193] Ibid., p. 55.

[194] Ibid., p. 57.

Other critiques addressed the choice of the discount rate for calculating net present benefits; the 'selection bias'; the use of *ex ante* estimates as a whole; the use of quantitative-only CBA; the scant attention to subgroups.[195] More recently, a report by Frontier Economics pointed to the fallacy of regulators in estimating welfare gains from new regulations, with specific reference to the UK Competition Commission's regulation of mobile termination charges.[196]

All these critiques raised doubts on the reliability and usefulness of CBA as a guide to policy-makers. Well-known commentators such as Cass Sunstein and Bob Hahn have explicitly responded to these issues in their recent publications.[197] In particular, Hahn extensively illustrated that the use of scorecards and economic analysis provides useful information on the effectiveness of regulatory policies; sets the stage for smarter regulation; facilitates oversight as well as the development of methods to assess the quality of regulation; promotes accountability and transparency in the policy-making process; and provides useful input for developing new research insights.[198]

Already in 2002, the OIRA received complaints by academicians suggesting that the OIRA should revise its approach to cost-benefit analysis. For example, a letter from the University of Texas to Frank Morrall recalled that a "number of academics have published devastating critiques of the current use of cost-benefit analysis in public health and environmental regulation ... We urge OMB to review these critiques and revise its approach to cost-benefit analysis

---

[195] See C. Sunstein, *Risk and Reason: Safety, Law and the Environment*, Cambridge: Cambridge University Press, 2002, and R.W. Hahn, *In Defense of the Economic Analysis of Regulation*, American Enterprise Institute, Washington, D.C., 2005.

[196] See Frontier Economics, "Wrong Numbers – Difficulties in Estimating the Welfare Gains from Regulation", *Bulletin*, June 2005.

[197] Another line of (at least partial) defence for cost-benefit analysis comes from the law and economics literature. In particular, Eric Posner has performed valuable work in explaining how a wide use of CBA can help the executive in overseeing agency discretion. Posner also argued that CBA reduces the possible influence of interest groups, thereby reducing the risk of regulatory capture. However, he also finds that the use of CBA is in most cases instrumental, in that agencies will perform a detailed CBA only when it is in the President's interest. Furthermore, CBA is found to have increased the amount of regulation, including regulation that fails a CBA test. See Eric A. Posner, "Controlling Agencies with Cost-Benefit Analysis: A Positive Political Theory Perspective", *University of Chicago Law Review*, Vol. 68, 2001, p. 1137.

[198] See Hahn, *In Defense of the Economic Analysis of Regulation*, op. cit.

accordingly".[199] An OIRA circular in September 2003 acknowledged that "[w]hen important benefits and costs cannot be expressed in monetary units, BCA is less useful, and it can even be misleading, because the calculation of net benefits in such cases does not provide a full evaluation of all relevant benefits and costs."[200]

Today, the debate on the relevance and reliability of quantitative techniques in impact assessment has not reached the final word. The dispute, however, seems to hinge more on the inherent limits of CBA in the quantification of net benefits for public health and environmental regulation, than on the usefulness of CBA in and of itself. CBA and CBA-based scorecards have proven quite useful in facilitating a comparative analysis of the efficiency and methodological soundness of regulatory impact assessments performed by agencies. Moreover, they have sent a signal to legislatures, emphasising that placing great emphasis on the neutrality of *ex ante* and *ex post* evaluation is hardly sustained by empirical evidence on the methods currently used by agencies in estimating prospective net benefits of new and existing regulations. OIRA itself included separate sections in its RIA Guide on measuring the cost-effectiveness of public health and safety regulations, as well as on the calculation of distributional effects, thus responding to most of the above-mentioned critiques.

Thus, once and again, the US experience seems to demonstrate that CBA is not a panacea, and that a 'one-size-fits-all' method that easily adapts to sectoral, economic, social and environmental regulations is nowhere to be found. As a consequence, a careful and gradual introduction of sector-specific impact assessment techniques would eventually solve many of the issues raised by scholars in criticising the current emphasis on quantitative CBA. See below, under Roadmap 3, for a discussion of sector-specific *ex ante* impact assessment.

A second methodological concern is related to evidence that lead DGs almost never compare alternative options in the observed ExIAs. In most of the ExIAs conducted in the 2003-05 period, DGs carried out the assessment after selecting the most preferred option. As a result, the impact assessment exercise relies on an 'educated guess' or more simply on a rule of thumb.[201] The subsequent assessment of the (already) chosen option, then, is useful

---

[199] See the letter to OIRA Director John Morrall by John Applegate and Wendy Wagner, 24 May 2002
http://www.whitehouse.gov/omb/inforeg/comments/comment100.pdf – retrieved 28 December 2005).

[200] See OIRA Circular D-4, 17 September 2003.

[201] The term 'educated guess' is borrowed from B. Lussis, *EU Extended Impact Assessment Review*, op. cit.

only as an indication of estimated costs for administrations and businesses or as a basis for consultation, but it does not provide any guidance in the selection of the most appropriate option for solving the problem at hand. A likely improvement in the quality of performed ExIAs would be achieved if a *quali-quantitative comparison of available alternatives is made mandatory, at least for major regulations*, without performing impact assessment after the preferred option has already been chosen with a *prima facie* approach.

Thirdly, the increasingly strong focus on reducing administrative burdens as one of the top priorities of EU better regulation clashes with the scant attention paid to administrative burdens by DGs in ExIAs. This problem is being tackled during the UK Presidency, based on the outstanding work recently done in the UK by the Better Regulation Task Force and the Better Regulation Executive on the issue of reducing administrative burdens.[202] As explained in section 2.3 above, the Commission is now turning back to the goal of streamlining existing legislation and avoiding regulatory hysteresis. Therefore, there seem to be encouraging prospects for *mandating that DGs assess the impact of alternative options also in terms of their potential to contrast regulatory creep and reduce compliance costs*.

Fourthly, and most importantly, the lack of methodological soundness in the Commission's ExIAs could be reduced by appointing an *ad hoc* agency in charge of cooperating with DGs in the drafting of impact assessment and to act as a help desk for all problems faced by lead DGs in quantifying the economic, social or environmental impact of proposed regulations.[203] As regards the likely impact on methodological soundness, a possible suggestion would be to *require that an external oversight agency cooperates with lead DGs in the drafting of ExIA, consults on quantitative analysis and suggests the rejection of the proposed regulation in case of insufficient or unsatisfactory ExIA.*

These are only some of the many ways in which the IIA methodology can be improved. Another important suggestion is to *promote the use of discount rates*. The analysis of the 70 ExIAs completed so far by the Commission reveals that DGs simply do not consider discounting future benefits, or calculating the net present value of future benefits. Only in two cases was the discount rate specified, and in both cases the assessment was

---

[202] See *supra*, section 1.2.2.

[203] Roadmap 10 below deals with this issue more extensively.

carried out by commissioning external studies.[204] Although the issue of benefit discounting is currently subject to debate (see Box 1), there is a wide consensus on the merit of choosing a reasonable social discount rate for calculating the present value of benefits from new regulations.[205] The choice of an appropriate discount rate allows a better comparison of alternative policy options, especially when regulators are faced with some options whose impact will be felt over differing time horizons. The Commission has recommended the use of a 4% discount rate, although the exact measure of such a rate deserves further attention.[206]

Moreover, the need to streamline existing regulation also calls for further emphasis on *including soft law and methods of self- and co-regulation* in the range of available alternatives. Since no external oversight agency is currently in charge of supervising the impact assessment conducted by DGs and *no sanctions are expressly provided* for insufficient or unsatisfactory assessments, there seem to be insufficient incentives for lead DGs to undertake difficult analyses such as the assessment of the expected impact of self-regulatory options.[207] With the creation of an *ad hoc* oversight agency with similar functions and powers to those of the US OIRA or the UK National Audit Office, the EU's stated ambition to de-ossify most EU

---

[204] See Lee and Kirkpatrick, op. cit. (fn 159 and accompanying text).

[205] See e.g. Arrow et al., op. cit., stressing that "[k]ey variables include the social discount rate ... Given uncertainties in identifying the correct discount rate, it is appropriate to employ a range of rates. Ideally, the same range of discount rates should be used in all regulatory analyses". See also R.W. Hahn, *In Defense of the Economic Analysis of Regulation*, American Enterprise Institute, Washington, D.C., 2005, p. 6 (stating that economists generally agree that some kind of discounting should be used in cost-benefit analyses, and that "the discount rate is critical in cost-benefit analysis".

[206] See the Commission's Technical Annex to the June 2005 Impact Assessment Guidelines, COM(2005)971, at note 90 and accompanying text. The Commission specifies that "This rate (4%) broadly corresponds to the average real yield on longer-term government debt in the EU over a period since the early 1980s." On the other hand, Robert Hahn employed rates ranging from 3% to 7%, whereas Frank Morrall tended to use higher rates, up to 10%.

[207] On the advantages and disadvantages of self-regulation, see e.g. R. Van Den Bergh, *Towards Efficient Self-Regulation in Markets for Professional Services* (available at *http://www.hertig.ethz.ch/LE_2005_files/Papers/Van_den_Bergh_Self-Regulation.pdf* – last accessed 7 December 2005).

legislation and substantially reduce the *acquis* would become more attainable.[208]

Table 1 summarises the recommendations included in Roadmap 1.

Table 1. Recommendations on Roadmap 1 - Methodology
1.1 Increase use of quantitative analysis.
1.2 Increase quali-quantitative comparison of available alternatives.
1.3 Enable assessment of regulatory creep and compliance costs.
1.4 Create an independent oversight agency as consultant, supervisor and regulatory clearinghouse.
1.5 Increase the use and consistency of discount rates.
1.6 Mandate inclusion of soft law, self- and co-regulation in the alternatives.
1.7 Introduce sanctions for insufficient or unsatisfactory IA.
1.8 Increase reliance on external expertise.

3.2 Roadmap 2 – Understanding and applying proportionality

The proportionality principle is one of the major pillars of the EU IIA model, and was expressly mentioned by the 2002 Communication on Impact Assessment as one of the guiding principles of the assessment exercise.[209] Emphasis on the proportionality principle was added by the Inter-Institutional Agreement on Better Lawmaking of December 2003.[210] Unfortunately, a precise definition of what is to be understood as 'proportionality' was not provided in the Commission background documents on impact assessment. The Guidelines and the Technical Annex to the 2002 Communication only provided a rather obscure definition, limited to guidance to DGs on 'getting things in proportion'. The 2002 Guidelines specified that the lead DG is in charge of defining how the principle of proportionate analysis applies to the proposal at hand, and that

---

[208] See e.g. the Commission Report, "Better Lawmaking 2004", COM(2005)98, 21 March 2005 ("Simplification of the *acquis* remains a top priority, in particular for the Lisbon strategy").

[209] See the 2002 Communication on Impact Assessment, COM(2002)276, section 3.2.c, stating that the "principle of proportionate analysis will be the driver of the [Impact Assessment] process".

[210] See *supra*, note 148 and accompanying text

the "form, content, volume and degree of detail" of ExIAs "will vary widely according to the nature of the proposal and its expected significance".[211]

As a matter of fact, the Commission realised that the first two years of implementation of the IIA model were characterised by a poor understanding of the principle of proportionate analysis. The 2004 progress report stated that "[t]he principle of proportionate analysis is to be better applied in practice", specifying that "the analysis has to focus on the most significant impacts and the most important distributive effects, and the depth of analysis has to match the significance of the impacts. Impact Assessments of proposals with no major impacts should, therefore, be avoided or at least kept short". The same report also highlighted the need for further guidance on the application of this principle, and stressed that "[t]he level of analysis needed will, for example, be easier to decide with increased transparency and better planning upstream of the impact assessment process".[212]

Some clearer guidance on how to apply the principle of proportionality while conducting an Extended Impact Assessment was provided in the updated Guidelines issued in June 2005. The new Guidelines specify that the principle of proportionate analysis implies that "the more significant an action is likely to be, the greater the effort of quantification and monetisation that will generally be expected. Besides, depending on the political and legal nature of the proposal under preparation, its sectoral particularities and the point in the policy-making process at which the IA is undertaken, some aspects of the analysis will often have to be developed more than others".[213] The Commission then clarifies that:

- The ExIA must be particularly developed whenever the proposal addresses an entirely new area or an area that was previously left to member states.

- The ExIA should not be too detailed when proposals aim at reviewing existing legislation. In this case, the analysis should focus

---

[211] See the Guidelines in the 2002 Communication on impact assessment, op. cit., p. 13.

[212] See the 2004 Progress Report, in the Commission Staff Working Party, *Impact Assessment: Next Steps*, op. cit., p. 5.

[213] See the 2005 Impact Assessment Guidelines, op. cit., p. 8.

on whether the available policy options are effective and versatile (meaning that they will adapt to future changes).

- In case of ExIAs on White Papers, Action Plans, other Communications setting out strategic orientations or proposed framework directives, the analysis will be 'rather broad', the IA will necessarily be preliminary and not quantitative.

- ExIAs will use already available estimates when they concern the proposed extension or renewal of existing programmes, and will use evidence on the impact of past comparable programmes in case they concern new expenditure programmes. The Commission clearly states that "[i]nformation about the impact of past activities will often be more convincing in this context than speculation about expected impacts."[214]

In the Annexes to the 2005 Guidelines, the Commission more directly invites DGs to apply the proportionality principle in deciding whether to monetise minor costs or benefits: "don't devote a lot of energy to putting a value on non-marketed impacts if they are a very small part of the overall impacts".[215]

It must be recalled that the proportionality principle can be given two different and complementary interpretations in the EU context:

- On the one hand, the so-called 'treaty-based' proportionality principle entails that the chosen policy option is adequate and not excessive to tackle the issue at stake, and can incorporate both a cost-effectiveness assessment and a compliance cost assessment, meaning that action undertaken at EU level should not impose unnecessary burdens on administrations, industry stakeholders and society as a whole.

- On the other hand, the 'methodological' principle of proportionate analysis focuses on the level of detail of impact assessment and postulates that the effort in quantifying and monetising impacts should be made directly dependent on the type and relevance of the proposal at hand.

The Commission seems to refer to the latter principle in providing guidance to DGs, but then appears to revert to the former in prescribing

---

[214] Ibid.

[215] See ibid., Technical Annex to the Guidelines, p. 37.

that DGs perform detailed regulatory impact assessments of new regulations, by ensuring that policy options do not go beyond what is necessary to achieve the objectives.[216] The major methodological questions, therefore, remain: When should an in-depth quantitative analysis be undertaken, and when is qualitative assessment a proportionate choice with respect to the type of proposal and the magnitude of the expected impact?

A first way to improve the use of proportionate analysis is certainly *the introduction of thresholds*. Just as in the US and the UK, lead DGs might be called upon to perform a detailed assessment of prospective benefits and costs of a proposed regulation only when the latter is expected to exert a substantial impact on the EU economy or, alternatively, when it has the potential to significantly affect the EU agenda or key policy priorities in subsequent years.[217] As was recalled in section 2.2, the Parliament's 'Doorn motion' envisaged the introduction of thresholds for impact assessment on 'major amendments' by the Council and the Parliament.

Secondly, the Commission should *issue more specific guidelines on how to assess compliance with the proportionality principle*. To ensure compliance with the Treaty-based proportionality principle, instead of merely stating that the principle of proportionate analysis "should be the driver of the process", the IIA model should require a detailed illustration of the reasons why less invasive regulatory options (e.g. self-regulatory options) have been discarded. Lead DGs should be required to ascertain that: i) the means employed are suitable for the purpose of achieving the objectives (effectiveness test); and ii) these means do not go beyond what is necessary to achieve the objectives (efficiency test).[218] Moreover, the Commission's guidelines should specify the criteria that should inspire the lead DG in choosing among the following options: i) perform a detailed quali-quantitative assessment of a range of policy alternatives, and then a

---

[216] See ibid., section 5, p. 8.

[217] An example of clear application of the methodological proportionality principle is provided by the Danish model of impact assessment. In Denmark, cost-benefit analysis is required only with respect to regulations that include major public construction projects, and the results of such analysis are then used as inputs to the RIA procedure.

[218] See e.g. the Report on developments in European Union procedures and practices relevant to parliamentary scrutiny issued by COSAC (Conference of Community and European Affairs Committees of Parliaments of the European Union), 30 April 2004.

detailed quantitative assessment of the prospective net benefits of the most preferred option; ii) perform a qualitative comparison of the available alternatives, and then a more detailed quantitative assessment of the prospective net benefits of the most preferred option; iii) quantify net benefits only for the preferred option, selected through a qualitative assessment; and iv) identify the preferred option only on the basis of a qualitative analysis.

Furthermore, an effective implementation can only be ensured if the Commission clearly states that *whenever ExIAs will not carry a justified application of the Treaty-based proportionality principle, they will be rejected as incomplete.* The introduction of a sanction mechanism would prove crucial for disciplining the lead DGs in acting consistently with one of the key principles of the whole IIA model. Likewise, in co-decision procedures, the *Council and the Parliament* might also state that they *will not consider any proposal from the Commission if it does not adequately take into account the Treaty-based proportionality principle.*[219]

Finally, as already mentioned in the previous section, the actual implementation of the methodological proportionality principle would be facilitated by the creation of an independent oversight agency, with the power to challenge ExIAs that fail to comply with the Commission guidelines on how to choose the appropriate depth of analysis. An oversight agency might also intervene at an early stage of the impact assessment exercise, in order to consult with sponsoring DGs on

---

[219] In the case of the Parliament, such a provision might reduce the costs associated with the subsequent scrutiny provided for in Art. 5 of the "Protocol on the application of the principles of subsidiarity and proportionality", OJ C310/207, 16 December 2004 ("Draft European legislative acts shall be justified with regard to the principles of subsidiarity and proportionality. Any draft European legislative act should contain a detailed statement making it possible to appraise compliance with the principles of subsidiarity and proportionality. This statement should contain some assessment of the proposal's financial impact and, in the case of a European framework law, of its implications for the rules to be put in place by Member States, including, where necessary, the regional legislation. The reasons for concluding that a Union objective can be better achieved at Union level shall be substantiated by qualitative and, wherever possible, quantitative indicators. Draft European legislative acts shall take account of the need for any burden, whether financial or administrative, falling upon the Union, national governments, regional or local authorities, economic operators and citizens, to be minimised and commensurate with the objective to be achieved.").

preliminary drafts and speed-up the assessment process by suggesting changes in the methodology chosen by the DG.

Suggestions on improving the application of the proportionality principle are summarised in Table 2.

Table 2. Recommendations on Roadmap 2 - Proportionality

2.1 Indicate proposals that require quantitative CBA of all alternatives.

2.2 Indicate proposals that require qualitative assessment of alternatives, and quantitative CBA of the selected option.

2.3 Indicate clearly when lead DGs can resort to cost-effectiveness, risk-risk or compliance cost analysis instead of CBA.

2.4 Appoint an external oversight agency in charge of supervising the application of the proportionality principle by lead DGs.

2.5 State that whenever ExIAs will not carry a justified application of the Treaty-based proportionality principle, they will be rejected as incomplete.

2.6 In case of co-decision procedures, the Parliament and the Council will not accept the proposal until it accounts for Treaty-based proportionality.

2.7 An external oversight agency should supervise the application of the methodological proportionality principle by lead DGs.

3.3 Roadmap 3 – Sector-specific impact assessment

Many of the problems encountered in the implementation of the IIA model can be traced back to the originally stated ambition to build a comprehensive integrated framework to be applied to several different types of regulatory initiatives, ranging from framework programmes to directives and regulations, and spanning fields with varying social, environmental and economic relevance. Defining a 'one-size-fits-all' model of impact assessment is no doubt an arduous task, and consensus on the need to provide for sector-specific assessment seems to be spreading amongst scholars and practitioners.

Further support to the idea of defining different IA models for different sectors comes from the scorecard illustrated in section 2.1. In particular, the analysis of ExIAs completed so far highlighted that some DGs appear to be less skilled than others in performing complex calculations on prospective costs and benefits. Moreover, some DGs are often called upon to perform specific assessments of non-marketable goods – e.g. the value of saved lives or life-years (VSL or VSLY), quality-adjusted life-years (QALY), the reduction of livestock, etc. Examples of DGs that have faced difficulties in performing complex calculations are DG FISH in the assessment of Council regulations establishing measures for the recovery of the southern hake stock and the Norway lobster stocks in the Cantabrian Sea and Western Iberian peninsula as well as the sole stocks in the Western Channel and the Bay of Biscay;[220] and DG AGRI in the assessment of the Regulation on support for rural development by the European Agricultural Fund and in the reviews of the sugar and tobacco regimes.[221] It is hard to imagine how the tools used for such assessments can be reconciled with those needed to assess, say, the *i2010* Communication or the EC Directive on the interoperability of digital interactive television services.[222]

Given the different skills and needs existing in the various DGs, the requirement to fine-tune the methodology used would have to be supported, once more, by the *creation of an oversight agency* in charge of supervising the activity of the DGs and cooperating with them in the definition of a satisfactory methodology.

Such a new model of sector-specific impact assessment would initially require that the Commission *defines the 'modules' of its IIA model that should be made sector-specific*, while declaring those that will remain unchanged for all DGs. Each Directorate General (or group of DGs) will then have to propose its own methodology, in a *joint effort with the external oversight agency. Involvement of the European Regulators Group* would be needed for those regulations that will be implemented and enforced by National Regulatory Authorities (NRAs). The sector-specific methodologies will then be subject to *a period of public consultation* of at least 60 days, during which interested stakeholders will be allowed to submit their comments on the model chosen by the DG. Following the public consultation, the *ad hoc* agency and the DGs would start implementing the new methodology in sponsoring new regulations. The resulting sector-specific methodology would have to be subject to *periodic review*.

The expected impact of such a new 'modular' framework is of course hard to assess. From a theoretical viewpoint, increasing the specificity of methodologies used is likely to produce mixed consequences for the

---

[220] SEC(2003)1480 and SEC(2003)1481.

[221] SEC(2003)1022 and SEC(2003)1023.

[222] SEC(2003)717 and SEC(2003)1028.

viability of the Commission's IIA model. Possible shortcomings include: i) a loss of standardisation; ii) an increase in short-run administrative costs, since a new oversight agency will have to be appointed and each DG will have to develop its own 'modules' in the IIA procedure; and iii) an increase in transaction costs, since DGs will have to negotiate the new procedure with the *ad hoc* agency.

Possible beneficial effects, however, include: i) greater precision and awareness in the application of the methodology; ii) lower medium- and long-run administrative costs, since DGs will invest resources *una tantum* in developing their own 'modules', and will have to produce less effort overtime in trying to adapt the 'one-size-fits-all' model to their peculiar needs; iii) greater involvement of stakeholders at an early stage, i.e. in the definition of the methodology; iv) possibility of benchmarking and lesson-drawing between different DGs, as well as beneficial identification of best practices and virtuous competition between DGs; v) greater responsibility and accountability for each of the DGs, with beneficial effects on the development of a 'culture of assessment' within each DG; vi) expected gains in the efficiency and effectiveness of the procedures; and vii) flexibility, since the new model would avoid useless efforts in trying to quantify and/or monetise variables that play only a marginal role in the problem at hand, yet must be assessed under the prescriptions of the standardised IIA model (e.g. environmental and social impact, subsidiarity, sustainability, etc.).

Examples of sector-specific methodologies include the so-called 'new approach to appraisal' (NATA) developed in the UK to stimulate efficient decision-making in the transport sector, which takes into account environment, safety, economy, accessibility and integration as top priorities;[223] the Integrated Environmental Assessment (IEA) developed by

---

[223] The *New Approach to Appraisal* (NATA) provides a framework within which "impacts under the headings of environment, safety, economy, accessibility and integration can be taken into account by the decision-maker. The idea is that the decision-maker applies his or her own weights to the impacts recorded against 21 objectives and makes a judgment about the proposal's overall value for money. In reaching a decision about a proposal, it is intended that account is also taken of the distribution and fairness of the impacts, the affordability and financial sustainability of the proposal, and its practicality and acceptability to the public". See the Commission of Integrated Transport (*http://www.cfit.gov.uk/docs/2003/10year/secondresearch/ad.htm* – last accessed 7 December 2005).

the European Environmental Agency;[224] the Health Impact Assessment developed within the World Health Organization,[225] the crime-proofing models currently being developed for the purpose of "testing legislative proposals as regards the crime opportunities they might create";[226] and many other models, whose theoretical soundness is strengthened by their widespread application in most developed and developing countries.

But the most insightful example of sector-specific impact assessment is no doubt the publication, by UK sectoral regulators such as OFCOM, OFGEM and the FSA, of guidance documents in which the sector-specific methodology applied in *ex ante* assessment is explained and made subject to public consultation.[227] This new approach should be adopted also by

---

[224] See e.g. F.L. Toth, *Participatory integrated assessment methods - An assessment of their usefulness to the European Environmental Agency*, EEA Technical Report No. 64, European Energy Agency, 12 September 2001; and M. Pierce, *Computer-based models in integrated environmental assessment*, EEA Technical Report No. 14, European Energy Agency, 25 October 1999.

[225] See the HIA Guidance section on the WHO website (http://www.who.int/hia/about/guides/en/ - visited 5 December 2005). For a model of a sector-specific IA, see G. Donev, "Methodology for Regulatory Impact Assessment related to Occupational Safety and Health", paper presented at the International Seminar on Implementation of Regulatory Impact Assessment: Best Practices in Europe, 8-11 June 2004, AUBG, Blagoevgrad, Bulgaria.

[226] See, inter alia, the Communication from the Commission to the Council and the European Parliament, *The prevention of crime in the European Union - Reflection on common guidelines and proposals for Community financial support*, COM/2000/0786; for a more updated description of current research on crime-proofing and impact assessment, see T. Vander Beken, "Legislative crime proofing - Detection and evaluation of loopholes that offer opportunities for organised crime", paper presented at the first European Congress on developing public/private partnerships to reduce the harm of organised crime, Dublin, 21 November 2003 (available at *http://www.ircp.be/uploaded/dublin-21-11-2003.ppt* - last visited 5 December 2005).

[227] See e.g. OFGEM, *Guidance on Impact Assessment* (*http://www.ofgem.gov.uk/ temp/ofgem/cache/cmsattach/11688_14805.pdf*, revised June 2005 - accessed 5 December 2005); OFCOM, *Better Policy Making. Ofcom's Approach to Impact Assessment*, 21 July 2005 (available at *http://www.ofcom.org.uk/consult/policy_making/ guidelines.pdf* – last visited 7 December 2005); and FSA's N2+2 Review of Cost-Benefit Analysis, which included two elements: a report by National Economic Research Associates (NERA) on CBA methodologies, and a report by John Howell

Commission DGs, in order to proceed towards more sector-specific impact assessment. Industry stakeholders would also welcome an increased institutionalisation of such procedures in specific 'modules' of the IIA model.[228]

Within the European Commission, only one DG (SANCO) has taken action to develop its own approach to impact assessment. It did so by launching the so-called 'Scoping paper', a single document covering all the necessary information to discuss, launch and develop an initiative from conception up to submission for approval. A Scoping paper contains what is termed as a 'quick and dirty' Impact Assessment, as well as a delivery plan, and applies to all new legislative and non-legislative initiatives leading to a Commission decision, with the sole exception of recurrent decisions or reports, routine comitology acts and technical measures deriving from already enacted legislation.[229] Such a new tool, launched in September 2005, is certainly to be welcomed as a step forward in the introduction of a culture of impact assessment in the Commission. However, it will be used more as a means to achieve greater homogeneity, awareness and transparency in the regulatory process, than as a way to increase the control on the prospective benefits and costs of yet-to-be-enacted regulation.[230]

Table 3 summarises some of the suggestions illustrated for introducing sector-specific impact assessment within the general framework of the IIA model.

& Co (JHC) on embedding CBA more deeply in the FSA. Both reports are available at *http://www.fsa.gov.uk/Pages/Library/Other_publications/Miscellaneous/2004/ n2_review.shtml* (last accessed 7 December 2005).

[228] A possible objection lies in the Commission's plan to introduce a computerised system for facilitating the impact assessment exercise performed by lead DGs. However, the standard software produced by the Commission will probably be made open-source when submitted to DGs, and as such might be tailored – at least in some of its modules – to the specific methodologies developed by individual DGs.

[229] See *http://teamwork.intbase.com/0509_01/docs/SANCO_scoping.pdf* for explanations and guidelines on how to prepare a SANCO Scoping Paper.

[230] See also the presentations by Mattia Pellegrini and John Bell at the DG SANCO Impact Assessment event held in Brussels on 26 October 2005.

Table 3. *Recommendations on Roadmap 3 – Sector-specific impact assessment*

3.1 Define the modules of the IIA model that should be adapted to the sector.

3.2 Enable each DG to propose its own methodology.

3.3 Involve the ERG for assessments that will be carried out by NRAs.

3.4 Provide for supervision, consultancy and clearance by an external audit.

3.5 Open defined procedures to public consultations for at least 60 days.

3.6 Provide for review of the defined methodology every three years.

3.7 Enable benchmarking of methodologies and lesson-drawing between DGs.

3.4 Roadmap 4 – Internal consistency and cost-effectiveness

A more urgent issue in the implementation of the IIA model is promoting its inherent consistency and cost-effectiveness by streamlining the IA procedure and taking action to enhance its efficiency, performance and overall coordination. The need to streamline the procedure is made more urgent as the number of entities currently dealing with better regulation issues in EU institutions has skyrocketed over the past decade, providing an outstanding example of how regulatory hysteresis can lead to useless cost duplications, reduced accountability and high administrative costs.

Within the Commission, active bodies and projects include inter-service groups such as the Interservice Coordination Group, the Impact Assessment Working Group, the APM-SPP Group; administrations with horizontal mandates such as the Legal Advisers Group, the General Secretariat, DG ADMIN, DG RTD and an announced Expert Group on Impact Assessment, and administrations with sectoral mandates such as most DGs, the Internal Market Advisory Committee (IMAC) and its Expert Group on Better Regulation; but also the European Business Test Panel, the Red Tape Observatory, the SINAPSE project and stand-alone projects on regulatory quality indicators and legislative burdens.[231]

---

[231] A document issued by the Commission highlights the striking proliferation of uncoordinated initiatives on better regulation in the Commission, the Parliament and the Council. See European Commission Working Document, *Who is Doing What on Better Regulation at EU Level – Organisation Charts*, 1 July 2004 (available at *http://www.eipa.nl/Topics/EPMF/documents/EU_Who_is_who_Better_regulation_July_0 4_sh_update.doc* - accessed on 5 December 2005).

On the other hand, Council administrations devoted to better regulation include the Competitiveness Council, the General Affairs Council, the Economic and Financial Affairs Council, the Group of Ministers Responsible for Public Administrations, the High-Level Group on Competitiveness, the Working Group on Competitiveness and Growth, the Directors and Experts on Better Regulation, the Economic Policy Committee, the announced *Ad Hoc* Working Group on Better Regulation, the General Affairs Group and many others. Whereas in the Parliament, the Committee on Legal Affairs and Internal Market, the Committee on Constitutional Affairs, the Committee on Industry, External Trade, Research and Energy, the Directorates on External Relations, Internal Relations, and Legislative Coordination/Interinstitutional Relations all retain some competency on better regulation and impact assessment. Such an overlap of competencies and uncoordinated initiatives certainly does not contribute to the accountability, transparency or efficiency of the EU's plans to enhance the quality of regulation. Not a great result for initiatives aimed, inter alia, at streamlining existing legislation and simplifying the *acquis*.

In addition, perhaps one of the most enduring problems faced in fostering the responsiveness and accountability of competent administrations is the *absence of clear-cut sanction mechanisms* for cases of insufficient quality of impact assessment. From a principal-agent perspective, the existence of sanctions and oversight by an external entity is a crucial step on the way to establishing a fruitful and efficient alignment between the efficiency-bound incentives of the principal and the self-interest of the agent. Action is urgently needed for establishing a comprehensive system in which *an ad hoc agency is in charge of supervising and coordinating the many initiatives* on impact assessment that are currently undertaken at EU level. Proposals aimed at increasing the internal consistency of the IIA procedure, such as the three-tiered model of impact assessment contained in the Parliament's Doorn Motion (see section 2.2) might achieve the same objective, yet would probably entail an excessive duplication of costs and provide for a milder inter-institutional dialogue, given the need to appoint three different audit bodies.

The proposed *ad hoc* agency would also be called to *ensure the overall consistency* of the methodologies applied by lead DGs, the Parliament and the Council for all assessed proposals with the key priorities set at EU level. Such a centralised oversight would eventually create the conditions for issuing a yearly publication on the overall impact of major EU regulations, modelled on the US yearly report on the costs and benefits of regulation.[232]

Table 4. Recommendations on Roadmap 4 – Internal consistency

4.1   Introduce sanction mechanisms.

4.2   Appoint a single *ad hoc* agency for the supervision of initiatives.

4.3   The agency will also supervise methodological consistency.

4.4   The agency will be in charge of reporting on overall impact of regulations.

3.5   Roadmap 5 – Increase the clarity of presentation

The current implementation of the Commission's IIA model exhibits fairly limited transparency, although the pervasiveness of the consultation process is probably the most encouraging achievement in the Commission's better regulation action plan. In some cases, the transparency of the ExIA exercise is already jeopardised by the nature of the proposal to be assessed – an example being certainly the "proposal amending the amended proposal for a decision amending Decision No. 1692/96/EC on the trans-European transport network".[233] Possible improvements in the transparency of the overall process as well as of the individual ExIA forms include better quality and clarity of presentation, better drafting, greater compliance with the IIA standard model and greater comprehensiveness of the ExIA forms.

First, the ExIAs are often obscure in the presentation of the methodology and the results. In many cases, the *comparison between identified costs and benefits has to be inferred* from the DG's explanations, with no clear reference to the justification for undertaking one of the options. Moreover, *some ExIAs are drafted half in English and half in French*, and present puzzling statements that undermine the general public's understanding of the grounds for intervention and for choosing a policy option.[234] Finally, the *use of comprehensive executive summaries* (included only in 10 out of 70 ExIAs) should be made mandatory. Executive summaries

---

[232] See section 1.1.

[233] See SEC(2003)1060.

[234] See also Lussis, op. cit.

should include a description of the methodology, tables summarising the qualitative or quantitative assessment performed, a summary of the consultation process and a description of the policy alternative undertaken and of its overall expected impact.

Secondly, DGs should strictly *adhere to the format outlined by the Commission Guidelines* while drafting ExIAs. Although most ExIAs observed follow at least some sections of the standard IIA form (i.e. description of the issue at stake, policy options available, stakeholder consultation and final Commission proposal), other sections are often willingly neglected.

Thirdly, the lead DGs seldom report quantitative calculations emerging from external studies, which are in most cases the only available source of cost-benefit analysis for the assessment of alternative policy options. An example is the ExIA on the "Communication on an Action plan for the implementation of the legal framework for electronic public procurement", for which costs and benefits were assessed through several external studies, but most figures were not reported in the final ExIA document.[235] A complete ExIA is supposed to *directly report the results of external studies*, without forcing the reader to consult those studies to find out about the reasons that led the DG to choose one alternative option over the others.

Finally, and needless to say, streamlining the procedure (roadmap 4) and *appointing an ad hoc agency* for impact assessment (roadmap 10) would provide the IIA model with an increased potential for supervising and controlling the transparency of the process. Table 5 summarises all the suggestions for roadmap 5.

Table 5. Recommendations on Roadmap 5 – Clarity of presentation

5.1 Always perform comparison between costs and benefits.

5.2 Improve clarity in the drafting.

5.3 Use comprehensive executive summaries.

5.4 Follow the standard IIA form.

5.5 Include the results obtained through external studies in the ExIA document.

---

[235] See SEC(2004)1639.

Roadmap 6 – Boosting cultural change

Emphasis on better regulation and the importance of impact assessment emerged as a result of the waves of public administration reforms that were introduced in some OECD countries during the 1970s and early 1980s. In particular, the UK *New Public Management* experience and the US *National Partnership for Reinventing Government* created fertile ground for the introduction of better policy-making tools, increased accountability of public administrations, greater transparency of the regulatory process and, more generally, higher responsiveness on the part of the regulators. The economic theory of organisation and the game-theoretical approach to policy-making as a principal-agent relationship suggest that better regulation initiatives are not likely to produce actual results unless accompanied by a parallel cultural shift, aimed at creating accountable and performance-oriented agents and promoting a 'culture of assessment'.

The Commission has initially underestimated the importance of training programmes as a tool to ensure responsible application of the IIA model. Only recently, an increased number of officials were reported to be receiving training organised by both the General Secretariat and individual DGs. The overall training system, however, seems still uncoordinated and is often left to the spontaneous initiative of individual units.

Cultural change within administrations can be promoted in at least three different ways. First, *training should be further coordinated*. Secondly, *DGs can be involved in the development of their own methodologies* (as described in Roadmap 3). Finally, all measures directed towards increasing the transparency and accountability of the IIA model (discussed in Roadmap 5), and particularly the *introduction of stronger oversight and control* can stimulate cultural change in administrations. Under a principal-agent approach, by adding oversight and monitoring mechanisms, agents (the DGs) internalise the externalities deriving from their behaviour, and thus have an incentive to behave efficiently in performing *ex ante* impact assessment.[236]

Table 6 summarises the above-mentioned suggestions.

---

[236] See e.g. J.E. Lane, *Public Principals and their Agents*, available at *http://www.spp.nus.edu.sg/docs/wp/wp32.pdf* (accessed 5 December 2005), and, more in general, J.J. Laffont and D. Martimort, *The Theory of Incentives: The Principal-Agent Model*, Princeton, NJ: Princeton University Press, 2002.

Table 6. Recommendations on Roadmap 6 – Promoting cultural change

6.1 Coordinate training initiatives.

6.2 Involve DGs in the development of methodologies.

6.3 Introduce control mechanisms for insufficient assessments.

3.6 Roadmap 7 – Strengthening *ex post* monitoring and evaluation tools

As widely acknowledged in the economic literature, an *ex ante* impact assessment model is not a sufficient tool for ensuring the quality of legislation. Methods for the *ex post* assessment of the effectiveness of IA models are being introduced in most OECD countries, and in a few cases have already shown encouraging results. *Ex post* assessment, moreover, is crucial for the adoption of a longer-term view on the responsiveness of regulators, a type of approach that is certainly needed at EU level for achievement of ambitious goals such as those stated in Lisbon. Policy tools for *ex post* evaluation and monitoring are currently underdeveloped in the EU, although the Commission has tendered a comprehensive external study on quality indicators, which will allegedly provide some guidance on how to monitor RIA compliance and performance. The review of the IIA model scheduled for early 2006 should make use of sophisticated tools for evaluating *ex post* the quality of the ExIAs conducted in the 2003-05 period.

A first way to implement *ex post* monitoring is to *introduce some form of compliance testing*. In line with the definition provided in a recent OECD report, compliance testing is a process-focused approach that implies verifying whether, in implementing the IIA model, lead DGs have met the procedural requirements set out in the Commission's Communications and guidelines on impact assessment.[237] Once discrepancies are found – as is likely to be the case for the IIA model – the competent authority should also *investigate the reasons for non-compliance* by lead DGs. Such reasons might range from the novelty and experimental nature of the procedure to difficulties in the quantification or monetisation of benefits or costs, but might also include political pressure directed at hindering the comprehensiveness of IIAs and cultural resistance by public officials.

---

[237] See OECD, *Regulatory Performance: Ex Post Evaluation of Regulatory Tools and Institutions*, Paris, September 2004, p. 21.

Examples of compliance tests used by regulators in OECD countries include, in part, the review of 48 RIAs completed between 1996 and 1999 by Robert Hahn and Patrick Dudley;[238] the National Audit Office's evaluation of RIA compliance between the 1998-2002 and the 2002-03 time frames, and subsequent compendium reports;[239] compliance testing introduced by the Swedish NNR (Board of Industry and Commerce for Better Regulation).[240]

In the case of the IIA model, however, compliance testing is likely to be an insufficient tool for a full evaluation of the quality of ExIAs. A more effective tool for evaluating the impact of the IIA model is the use of output-focused *performance tests*. Such tests are geared towards measuring the quality and consistency of undertaken ExIAs, more than mere compliance with pre-defined requirements. Although more resource-intensive, such tests can provide useful guidance for both taking stock and looking forward to improvements in the IIA model. According to a recent OECD survey, performance tests are the most widely adopted form of *ex post* evaluation, with the UK, Netherlands and Sweden being amongst the international best practices.[241] Performance tests can take many forms, ranging from survey-based analysis of IA quality to tests aimed at assessing the differences between the actual effects of regulations and the effects that had been predicted *ex ante* in the IA document.

The use of performance testing also enables *the identification of best and worst practices* amongst administrations in charge of performing impact assessment. In the UK, for example, after an extensive review of RIAs performed by the NAO in the 2000-2002 timeframe, the Chairman of the Better Regulation Task Force, David Arculus, publicly called for further scrutiny on the activity of individual departments (most notably, the Home

---

[238] See Hahn and Dudley, op. cit.

[239] See National Audit Office, *Evaluation of Regulatory Impact Assessment Compendium Report 2004-2005*, Report by the Comptroller and Auditor General, HC 341 Session 2004-2005, 17 March 2005.

[240] See N. Munnich, *The Regulatory Burdens and Administrative Compliance Costs for Companies*, survey conducted by the Confederation of Swedish Enterprise, Brussels Office, April 2004.

[241] See e.g. W. Harrington, "RIA Assessment Methods", and W. Harrington and R.D. Morgenstern, "Evaluating Regulatory Impact Analyses", papers prepared for the OECD project on *ex post* evaluation of regulatory tools and institutions, OECD, Paris, 2003.

Office, the Department of Transport and the Department for Media, Culture and Sport) which had, in his opinion, performed particularly badly; whereas the Department of Trade and Industry was indicated as an example of good practice. Arculus also identified individual RIAs from which 'interesting lessons' could be learnt.[242] In the EU case, the best practice so far would probably be the ExIA performed for the INSPIRE Directive, at least according to the results of the scorecard presented in section 2.1.[243]

Moreover, the use of performance tests can *provide useful information on the timing of evaluations performed*. A reported example is that of the Netherlands, where an interview-based evaluation of RIA performance led to the conclusion that early involvement of a regulatory oversight body can add significantly to the effectiveness and timeliness of the overall procedure. Similar lessons would probably be drawn with respect to the European IIA model, in which a real oversight body has not been appointed.[244]

Finally, another form of performance testing is to *evaluate the actual cost of regulatory initiatives undertaken under a RIA regime*. The main goal pursued in using such tools is to evaluate whether the introduction of impact assessment has led to a reduction in the administrative costs of regulation. Examples include the administrative cost assessment conducted by the Danish Business Test Panels in the late 1990s;[245] but also Morgenstern's analysis of environmental regulatory programmes in the US;[246] and, most importantly, the *ex post* assessment of administrative burdens undertaken through the Standard Cost Model in the Netherlands,

---

[242] See the letter sent by David Arculus to the Comptroller and Auditor General, op. cit.

[243] Extended Impact Assessment of the proposed Directive establishing an infrastructure for spatial information in the Community, SEC(2004)980 (Directive COM(2004)516).

[244] See OECD, *Regulatory Performance*, op. cit., §97.

[245] See B. Hagerup, *Business Impact Assessment – The Danish Model* (available at *http://www.oecd.org/dataoecd/58/39/2410437.pdf);* and the section on Denmark at *http://europa.eu.int/comm/enterprise/enterprise_policy/best-directory/en/administration/denmark.htm* (visited 5 December 2005).

[246] R.D. Morgenstern, *Economic Analyses at EPA: Assessing Regulatory Impact*, Resources for the Future, Washington, D.C., 1997.

Denmark, Sweden and Norway, and currently under consideration in the UK and – under the UK Presidency – in the EU.[247]

Besides compliance and performance tests, scholars have also developed more *sophisticated tools known as 'function tests'*, whose main feature is the search for the actual contribution provided by impact assessment to the regulatory process. Function tests can include: i) the assessment of the frequency with which initial proposals are revised or abandoned as they progress through the process; ii) measures of the difference between initial proposals and finally adopted regulations; iii) 'audit trail' methods that focus on the measurement of changes in the initial proposal as well as on the treatment of such changes; and iv) survey-based methods to investigate the change in the administrative or regulatory culture fostered by RIA. Function testing can be expected to be significantly more resource-intensive and discretionary than performance testing. Perhaps forms of function tests that can be applied most usefully to the peculiar features of the IIA model are *ex post* measures of cultural change, as they stress the importance of monitoring increased awareness amongst public officials as an essential ingredient of a successful better regulation action plan. Examples of the use of such tests can be found in Canada and New Zealand, with encouraging results, and in Denmark, with more disappointing findings.

A final, important question is who should undertake *ex post* evaluation. Once more, both international experience and economics literature suggest that oversight by an independent body is key to the successful implementation of *ex post* evaluation. For example, the UK Better Regulation Task Force considers the Dutch experience on performance testing as showing clear evidence that "it is essential to have an independent body overseeing the Administrative Burden reduction effort", just like Actal does in the Netherlands.[248] More generally, compliance testing and performance testing should be scheduled on a periodic basis and performed by an independent governmental body, whereas function

---

[247] For a comprehensive list of sources and figures on the Dutch and international experience in calculating administrative burdens with the standard cost model, see *www.compliancecosts.com*; the UK attempt to apply the Dutch methodology for the purpose of reducing red tape is described above in footnotes 105-106 and accompanying text.

[248] See the *Less is More* White Paper by the BRTF, op. cit., section 3.

testing – essentially survey-based – should make use of external expertise and be left out of periodical reviews, as it might prove significantly more costly than compliance and performance testing.

At EU level, a pilot project on indicators of regulatory quality (IRQ) was launched in 2004 within the 2001-05 Multiannual Programme for Enterprise and Entrepreneurship. The project's Final Report, issued in December 2004, proposed the use of three systems of quality indicators: *i) macro and ex-ante indicators*, focusing on the design of better regulation tools and policy; *ii) micro and ex-post indicators*, more outcome-focused and to be implemented in countries where stakeholder consultation is already an established practice; and *iii) systems of quality assurance* aimed at bridging the (technical) measurement of regulatory quality and the (political) evaluation of better regulation as public policy.[249] The results of the project, *if implemented systematically through the Commission's legislative cycle, would allow for significant improvements* in the monitoring of EU legislation, as well as in the fight against red tape. However, a lot still needs to be done to ensure that the articulated *corpus* of EC legislation is scrutinised in terms of output, outcomes and administrative costs.

An attempt to monitor administrative burdens at member state level is contained in the Final Report of the Pilot Project "Ex-Post Evaluation of EC Legislation and its Burden on Business", published in May 2005.[250] The project considered a sampling of directives – the construction sites Directive, the medical devices Directive, the IPPC (integrated pollution prevention and control) Directive and the product safety Directive – and analysed their transposition into national legislation in eight EU member states.[251] The main results of the survey were presented by reporting the share of existing companies that would have cancelled or down-scaled their activities in the absence of regulation – an approach that reveals the real focus of the project, i.e. exploring the extent to which target firms have welcomed the regulation. The results showed that a significant share of the companies find that the requirements of at least two of the analysed

---

[249] See the pilot project's website (*http://www.brad.ac.uk/irq/* - visited on 5 December 2005).

[250] Final Report of the Pilot Project "Ex-Post Evaluation of EC Legislation and its Burden on Business", published in May 2005 by the European Commission, Enterprise DG.

[251] The member states considered were Denmark, France, Germany, Greece, the Netherlands, Poland, Spain and the UK.

directives (the construction sites Directive and the medical devices Directive) are burdensome and do not add any important value to their business processes in the field. Insufficient data were gathered for the IPPC Directive, while results were more encouraging for the product safety Directive.

Such an approach, of course, seems hardly suitable for new pieces of legislation – such as the product safety Directive – which inevitably impose new burdens on regulated firms, irrespective of whether such burdens can be passed-on downstream to final consumers.[252] Moreover, the methodology used to capture the impact of transposed Directives on health, safety and the environment should significantly depart from that used to measure the extent to which firms remain disappointed by a new 'protectionist' measure. In other words, regulatory burdens are not always bad, although useless burdens certainly are. The sample of directives chosen and the scope of the analysis, therefore, appear too limited; this, in turn, calls for a better fine-tuning of the tools used for sampling the perception of firms faced with the transposition of EC directives into national legislation.

Table 7 summarises the suggestions for undertaking *ex post* monitoring and evaluation of the IIA model.

Table 7. Recommendations on Roadmap 7 – Ex post monitoring and evaluation

7.1 Introduce methods of compliance testing.

7.2 Investigate reasons for non-compliance.

7.3 Enable performance testing.

7.4 Follow the recommendations of the IRQ Pilot Project.

7.5 Identify and publish best and worst practices.

7.6 Appoint independent body to monitor administrative burdens.

7.7 Schedule periodic testing.

7.8 Use external expertise for *una tantum* survey-based tests of cultural change.

---

[252] See e.g. R. Craswell, "Passing on the Costs of Legal Rules: Efficiency and Distribution in Buyer-Seller Relationships", *Stanford Law Review*, No 43, 1991, p. 361.

3.7   Roadmap 8 – National RIA models: A new *Koine dialectos*?

As recently recalled by one authoritative commentator, the meaning of RIA can vary widely amongst the EU member states.[253] As impact assessment tools are conceived for strikingly different purposes and with differing levels of sophistication in member states, the potential of an improved EU IIA model to boost competitiveness in the EU25 could be significantly hindered by the heterogeneity of procedures adopted at member state level for the transposition of EU legislation as well as for the enactment of new national rules. As a result, the quality of a pan-European IIA strongly depends on both coordination and competition between RIA systems adopted at EU, national and sub-national levels.

From this standpoint, it would seem *prima facie* appropriate to provide for a standardisation of the IA procedure throughout all the EU25. However, a closer look reveals that RIA cannot be implemented as a standardised, 'one-size-fits-all' procedure for all individual member states. Each nation exhibits a peculiar business and social environment, as well as a different legislative *acquis*, which ultimately call for different criteria in conceiving, drafting and transposing regulations.

A quick look at impact assessment models adopted at member state level reveals a striking heterogeneity of approaches as well as a patchwork of regulatory initiatives often converging towards a common goal, i.e. fostering better regulation as a means to reduce administrative burdens, foster competitiveness and enable sustainable development. As regards impact assessment procedures, EU countries differ in many respects, including: i) the actual implementation of impact assessment; ii) the institutional setting in which assessment is performed; iii) the stage of legislative preparation/drafting at which impact assessments take place; iv) the degree of comprehensiveness of impact assessment models adopted;[254]

---

[253] See C. Radaelli, "How Context Matters: Regulatory Quality in the European Union", paper prepared for the special issue of the *Journal of European Public Policy* on Policy Convergence, 17 April 2004; and C. Radaelli, *What Does Regulatory Impact Assessment Mean in Europe?*, Working Paper No. 05-02, AEI-Brookings Joint Center for Regulatory Studies, Washington, D.C., January 2005.

[254] A good example of the different scope of RIA in EU countries is the type of the analysis required: as a matter of fact, while the Netherlands adopted a business effects analysis, which focused on the impacts arising from businesses, in the Czech Republic the analysis focuses on the financial and economic impacts, which has expanded to cover other socio-economic impacts. France adopted a General Impact Analysis, which specifically addresses employment and fiscal impacts,

v) the methodologies adopted for impact assessment, ranging from cost-effectiveness analysis to cost-benefit analysis, risk-risk analysis, assessment of procedural efficiency, qualitative techniques, etc.; vi) the use and timing of public consultation as an input to regulatory impact assessment, and in general the transparency of the procedures adopted; vii) the adoption of a so-called 'two-stage approach' to impact assessment, which entails the performance of both a preliminary and an extended impact assessment; viii) the use of *ex post* evaluation procedures; ix) the adoption of an integrated, multi-valued model of impact assessment such as that adopted in the EU; and x) the extent to which compatibility between national and EU legislation is taken into account; and many others.

First, as regards the implementation of impact assessment at national level, pioneering countries such as the UK, the Netherlands, Denmark, Sweden and Finland, seem to have already achieved a mature and effective model of regulatory impact assessment, although significant margins for improvement still exist. Likewise, other member states, such as Germany, Poland and Austria, recently took significant steps towards a more efficient assessment system, although it is probably too early to draw definitive conclusions in this respect. In contrast, Italy, Spain, Portugal, Greece and most accession states seem to lag behind, and remain in an experimental phase in the introduction of effective and pervasive models of impact assessment. In some cases, impact assessment is still at a stage of a declaration of intentions, whereas in other cases, RIA has gradually lost momentum after a period of initial thrust.[255]

Secondly, member states exhibit profound differences on other issues as well. On one extreme, countries such as the UK and Denmark seem to take into account all possible aspects of major regulations. In Denmark, for example, since 1995, assessing the impact of a proposed regulation requires three stages of analysis (screening, scoping and assessment) together with a mandatory assessment of the impact on competition, the environment and the relationship with EU legislation. Denmark adopted a multi-valued model which takes into account the economic, social and environmental impact of proposed regulations, and also developed *ex post* methods for

---

whereas Austria and Portugal only undertake fiscal analyses, which focus on the direct budgetary costs of government administration.

[255] See Radaelli, *What Does Regulatory Impact Assessment Mean in Europe?*, op. cit., p. 3.

evaluating the impact of selected regulations. The proportionality principle is broadly and effectively applied, so that cost-benefit analysis is used mostly in the evaluation of major public construction projects. The Danish model implies an extensive use of consultation and business test panels, normally before a bill is presented to the Parliament. Consultation is open to the general public and its results – like RIA results – are published on the Internet.[256]

At the other extreme, some EU member states seem to lag far behind in the adoption and effective implementation of impact assessment. This situation has emerged with further evidence after the enlargement process. Countries such as Slovenia, Bulgaria, Hungary and the Baltic states are currently following the EU and the OECD recommendations in the application of RIA, but have limited experience in the field of better regulation. Bulgaria and Romania, for example, had to face the overwhelming challenge of both a transition towards a market economy and the adoption of the *acquis communautaire*. Of course, the transition phase created enormous problems in the identification of possible market failures, since well-developed markets did not exist in most of these countries. Consequently, both the regulatory and (where separate) sustainability impact assessment procedures needed an *ad hoc* crafting. Urgent issues also included the establishment and institutional positioning of a Better Regulation Unit, considered as crucial for the monitoring and achievement of better regulation in those countries. Such units have to accomplish the delicate task of coordinating existing national legislation with the *acquis*, as well as that of ensuring that national and sub-national laws comply with minimum standards of transparency, accountability and methodological soundness.[257]

Another example is Slovakia, where RIA is currently being implemented. Many commentators recently stressed the absence of oversight, transparency, pervasiveness and public participation in the policy-making process in Slovakia, and the lack of specific training of public officials as one of the main obstacles towards the achievement of

---

[256] See *Regulatory Impact Analysis (RIA) Inventory*, op. cit., p. 20.

[257] See e.g. J. Kleinertova, "Specifics and Problems of RIA in Transition Economics and How to Overcome Them"; and J. Rajdlova, "Impact Assessment in a Country of Reforms – Slovak Experience", papers presented at the International Seminar on Implementation of Regulatory Impact Assessment: Best Practices in Europe, 8-11 June 2004, AUBG, Blagoevgrad, Bulgaria.

effective methods of assessing the impact of proposed regulations.[258] Political instability also contributed to the slow adoption of a satisfactory impact assessment model. In the case of Slovakia, a team of Dutch and Slovak experts developed a set of Guidelines and a business impact assessment model within the MATRA pre-accession project, but the implementation of such project was then hindered by a change of government.

Even greater difficulties are associated with the implementation of impact assessment procedures in candidate countries. The EU stimulated adoption of RIA in candidate countries by inserting regulatory reform and impact assessment amongst the requirements to be fulfilled on the way to accession. International organisations such as the OECD and the World Bank and, in some cases, EU member states such as the UK are now supporting candidate countries in the development of effective RIA models. For example, the role of impact assessment in the EU-Turkey negotiations was the subject of a recent seminar held in Ankara in June 2005 within the OECD SIGMA project, where the content and purpose of regulatory impact assessment was illustrated to Turkish officials with a view to future implementation. The same applies to Croatia, where regulatory impact assessment was introduced only through a pilot project in 2004.[259]

The transplant of impact assessment models already implemented in EU member states will certainly prove delicate for candidate countries such as Ukraine. Moreover, each candidate country will face peculiar challenges in fulfilling its European ambition, leaving no room for single recipes, or even less comprehensive solutions that prove *bonnes à tout faire*.[260]

---

[258] See e.g. K. Staronova, *Analysis of the Policy-making Process in Slovakia*, 2003 (available at *http://www.policy.hu/staronova/FinalResearch.pdf*).

[259] Even outside the EU borders, regulatory impact assessment is a key item in negotiations undertaken by the EU in its external relations. For example, in the EU/Ukraine Action Plan, Ukraine committed to "adopt and implement a system of impact assessment of regulatory measures, consultation of stakeholders, and prior notification of regulatory changes to economic operators to ensure transparency (predictability of regulatory environment)". See EU/Ukraine Action Plan (*http://www.ieac.org.ua/pics/content/15/1109931048_ans.doc*, p. 7).

[260] The situation, however, is not confined within the boundaries of accession countries. Italy, for example, introduced RIA for a number of pilot projects in 2000, with overtly disappointing results. In 2001, the Presidency of the Italian

More recently, the European Commission has provided a snapshot of the current level of implementation of RIA at member state level. Figure 9 provides an overview of measures in the area of better regulation and impact assessment as reported by the Commission in its March 2005 Communication on Better Regulation for Growth and Jobs in the EU.[261] Although some of the Commission's findings might be questionable, the

Figure 9. Overview of measures in the area of better regulation and impact assessment

	Better Regulation Programme	Specific RIA Policy	Obligatory RIA	Alternative Instruments Considered	Guidelines for RIA	Coordinating Body for RIA	Consultation part of RIA	Formal Consultation procedures	Direct Stakeholder Consultation	Test of impact on Small Enterprises	Exemptions for SMEs	Total Y + (Y)
Belgium	(Y)	N.A.	(Y)	N.A.	(Y)	(Y)	N	(Y)	(Y)	(Y)	N	7
Czech Rep.	Y	N.A.	N	Y	N.A.	N.A.	N.A.	N.A.	N.A.	(Y)	N	3
Denmark	Y	Y	Y	Y	Y	Y	Y	Y	Y	Y	N	10
Germany	Y	N.A.	N.A.	N.A.	Y	Y	Y	Y	N.A.	N.A.	N.A.	5
Estonia	N	Y	Y	Y	N.A.	N.A.	N	N	N	N.A.	Y	4
Greece	(Y)	(Y)	N	N	N	N	Y	N	N	N	N.A.	3
Spain	Y	(Y)	Y	(Y)	(Y)	(Y)	N	N	N	N	N.A.	6
France	N.A.	N.A.	N.A.	N.A.	N.A.	N.A.	N.A.	N.A.	N.A.	N.A.	N.A.	0
Ireland	Y	N	N	(Y)	(Y)	N	(Y)	(Y)	N	N	N	5
Italy	(Y)	Y	N	(Y)	Y	(Y)	(Y)	N	Y	(Y)	N	8
Cyprus	N	N	N	N	N	N	N	N	N	N	N.A.	0
Latvia	Y	Y	Y	Y	Y	Y	Y	Y	N	Y	N	9
Lithuania	N.A.	Y	Y	Y	Y	N.A.	N.A.	N.A.	N	N.A.	N.A.	4
Luxembourg	Y	N.A.	Y	Y	N.A.	Y	Y	Y	N	N	Y	7
Hungary	Y	(Y)	Y	N	N	Y	(Y)	(Y)	N	N	N	6
Malta	Y	N.A.	N.A.	N	N.A.	(Y)	N	N	Y	N	Y	4
Netherlands	Y	Y	N.A.	Y	Y	Y	N	N	Y	(Y)	Y	8
Austria	Y	Y	Y	Y	Y	N	Y	Y	Y	N.A.	N	8
Poland	Y	Y	Y	Y	Y	Y	Y	Y	(Y)	N	Y	10
Portugal	N	N	N	N	N	N	N	N	N	N	N	0
Slovenia	Y	N.A.	N.A.	N.A.	N.A.	N.A.	N.A.	N.A.	N.A.	N.A.	N.A.	1
Slovakia	N.A.	N.A.	N.A.	N.A.	N.A.	N.A.	N.A.	N.A.	(Y)	N.A.	N	1
Finland	Y	Y	Y	Y	Y	(Y)	Y	Y	Y	N.A.	N.A.	9
Sweden	Y	Y	Y	Y	Y	Y	Y	Y	Y	N	N	9
UK	Y	Y	Y	Y	Y	Y	Y	Y	Y	Y	Y	10
Total Y + (Y)	19	13	12	15	15	14	12	12	11	7	5	

Source: *European Commission, Communicaton on Better Regulation for Growth and Jobs in the European Union, 16 March 2005*

Legenda

Y	Measures exist	(Y)	Measures available partially	N	Measures don't exist	N.A.	No info avaiable

Government issued a new Directive on RIA, which launched a new experimental phase and a comprehensive reform of the initially adopted RIA model, including also a careful reconsideration of the 'two-stage' approach. However, the results of the second experimental phase have been, if possible, even more worrying. Another example is Spain, where regulatory impact assessment is underdeveloped and cost-benefit analysis is replaced by a questionnaire composed by 20 questions on reasons for intervention, legal and institutional impact and social and economic impact. The Spanish model entails no *ex-post* scrutiny and no consultation.

[261] See section 2.3 above.

overall picture is crystal-clear on the patchwork of heterogeneous experiences that composes the EU mosaic on impact assessment.[262]

In summary, the persisting (and even widening) differences between impact assessment models adopted in EU member states call into doubt the likelihood that the EU's efforts towards better regulation will be effectively mirrored by efficient and effective national policies. And, as good quality regulation is considered to be a major step to achieving the ambitious Lisbon goals, further efforts are required in order to foster the convergence of impact assessment at member state level. Such efforts may include:

- *Improving the transposition process*, in particular by avoiding unnecessary 'gold-plating' of directives, which can impose harmful administrative burdens and excess regulation on targeted groups, and encouraging the adoption of 'light touch' regulatory options.

- *Establishing a common language on impact assessment*, in order to avoid the 'garbage can' fallacy.[263] This goal can be pursued, for example, by issuing a Communication on impact assessment performed at national level, in which the Commission could clarify the key principles that should inspire the IA exercise.[264]

- *Providing for gradual convergence on key issues* such as mandatory competitiveness-, subsidiarity- and proportionality-proofing, red tape screening, stakeholder consultation and calculation of net benefits of major proposals.[265]

---

[262] Similar findings emerge from the so called 'Rhodes Report'. See *Report to the Ministers responsible for Public Administration in the EU member states on the progress of the implementation of the Mandelkern Report's Action Plan on Better Regulation*, ad hoc Group of Directors and Experts on Better Regulation (DEBR), Athens, May 2003.

[263] See Radaelli, *What Does Regulatory Impact Assessment Mean in Europe?*, op. cit., observing that RIA is seen as a solution to different problems amongst EU countries. In particular, some countries (Germany, Sweden and Italy) see RIA as a solution to the problem of simplification, others (e.g. the Netherlands) as a tool to promote competitiveness, while still others (Denmark) link RIA to the quality of the business environment.

[264] Such a Communication could be linked to the National Lisbon Programmes, as implemented under the new "Recommendations for Actions to Member States for Inclusion in their Lisbon Programmes". See COM(2005)24, companion document, 3 February 2005.

[265] The UK Presidency of the European Union stated its intention to "reach

- *Creating a network of national RIA authorities*, coordinated by a new European independent oversight agency, in order to stimulate dialogue, knowledge dissemination and exchange of best practices amongst EU member states.[266]

All these efforts should be geared towards the definition of a 'common language' on impact assessment. Such endeavour should not, however, aim at erasing all contextual differences between national policy processes. Instead, the different 'RIA dialects' existing in the EU25 should be reconciled, leading to a *koine dialectos* that would certainly help the EU Better Regulation Action Plan achieve its ultimate goals. Table 8 summarises the suggestions for enabling a gradual convergence of RIA models at member state level.

Table 8. Recommendations on Roadmap 8 – Subsidiarity

8.1 Improve transposition.
8.2 Issue a communication on RIA in member states.
8.3 Provide for gradual convergence on key issues.
8.4 Create a network of national RIA authorities to be coordinated by a new independent oversight agency at EU level.

---

agreement among Member States and the Commission on a common methodology for the measurement of the administrative burden of legislation, which, once agreed, would be included in all impact assessments." See *Prospects for the EU in 2005 – The UK Presidency of the European Union*, presented to Parliament by the Secretary of State for Foreign and Commonwealth Affairs by Command of Her Majesty, June 2005, pp. 10-11. On establishing a common language on the need to calculate and maximise net benefits in Europe, see Hahn and Litan, *Counting Regulatory Benefits and Costs: Lessons for the US and Europe*, op. cit., p. 500. ("The European Union should implement a policy specifying that the primary objective of regulation is to maximize net benefits.")

[266] This initiative would draw on the work already done by the Mandelkern Group. The conclusions of the meeting of the Ministries of Public Administration at La Rioja in May 2002 required "that the Directors of Better Regulation and the Mandelkern Group experts continue to meet together on a regular basis under the name of Mandelkern Group on Better Regulation, ensuring the coherence of their work with the above-mentioned Action Plan. The group in question will report to the Ministers responsible for Public Administration and Better Regulation on the results of the implementation of better regulation tools in Member States and on the Action Plan." See the Rhodes Report, op. cit., p. 3.

3.8   Roadmap 9 – Issue guidelines on competitiveness-proofing and competition assessment

As recalled earlier, although the IIA model was initially rooted in sustainable development, it gradually became an important tool to facilitate the achievement of the competitiveness goal set at the Lisbon Council and re-launched in the wake of the Kok Report.[267] As a result, all IA exercises completed should ensure that the policy option undertaken will not harm the competitiveness of EU firms. In this respect, many stakeholders have underlined the need to provide for competitiveness-proofing of the proposals analyzed through preliminary impact assessment.

Further support to this idea came from the 'four presidencies initiative' launched on 26 January 2004, which proposed to introduce mandatory competitiveness-proofing of major new regulations by the Competitiveness Council (CC).[268] The Irish Presidency declared that it would ensure "that the policy proposals tested for their impact on competitiveness under the Commission Integrated Impact Assessment process will be considered at the Competitiveness Council leading to an effective system of 'competitiveness proofing' for proposed legislative measures."[269] Similar plans were formulated by the UK Presidency in setting its priorities for the July-December 2005 term.[270] However, it is still unclear what is meant by competitiveness-proofing. Such an oversight can take many different forms and intervene at different points in time. As regards the timing of intervention, possible options are:

- The CC can intervene in the choice of the regulatory option by suggesting the 'more competitiveness-oriented option';

---

[267] The Report of the High Level Group Chaired by Wim Kok, *Facing the Challenge,* presented in November 2004 (available at *http://europa.eu.int/growthandjobs/group/index_en.htm*).

[268] See *supra*, note 168.

[269] See the Report of the Irish Presidencies, *The Competitiveness Council Priorities Paper,* January 2004, p. 6.

[270] See *Prospects for the EU in 2005 – The UK Presidency of the European Union*, op. cit., p. 10. ("we must improve the policy making process with better consultation and impact assessments, which will include testing all regulatory proposals in the Commission's 2005 work programme for their impact on competitiveness").

- The CC takes part in the consultation process after the preferred option has already been chosen, but before the extended impact assessment is completed;
- The CC is consulted before the ExIA is drafted for an 'interim competitiveness-proofing';
- The CC is consulted for a 'final competitiveness check' after the ExIA document has been completed;
- The CC is consulted both at the preliminary stage and at the end of the impact assessment exercise; or
- The CC supervises the whole impact assessment process and retains the power to repeal any proposal that is likely to harm EU competitiveness.

Amongst these options, the ones in which the Competitiveness Council is called upon to supervise all the regulatory impact assessment process and/or to intervene at more than one stage appear probably too costly and burdensome, unless the CC is provided with more extensive powers to act as an independent body in charge of overseeing the overall quality of the methodology and procedure adopted by the lead DGs and other officials in charge of impact assessment. Economists and practitioners have stated the importance of involving oversight bodies at quite an early stage of the regulatory process, and in this respect the most preferred option should be to involve the CC in the choice of the regulatory option, so that the CC can suggest the most pro-competitive of the available alternatives. However, in this case the CC would not be able to actually perform a real check on the pro-competitive nature of the proposal undertaken. For this reason, the most effective timing for competitiveness-proofing is probably the interim stage following the preliminary IA and preceding the completion of the ExIA.

Concerning the form of intervention, possible options include:

- The CC grants a clearance to the proposed regulation by stating that it is not inconsistent with the goal of promoting EU competitiveness;
- The CC performs a detailed assessment of the impact of the proposal on EU competitiveness; or
- The lead DGs mandatorily report in the ExIA on the consistency of the preferred regulatory option with the goal of competitiveness; the CC only monitors to ensure that the lead DG has correctly performed this task. Competitiveness-proofing is included in the IIA model as a compulsory stage of the analysis and the CC (or an independent

body) is granted the power to mandate the review of ExIAs in case of insufficient compliance with the obligatory requirement.

Of the three above-mentioned options, the third seems to be probably more consistent with the target of streamlining the IIA procedure. First, it would reduce transaction costs between lead DGs and the CC. Secondly, it would reduce uncertainty for DGs in drafting the ExIAs. Thirdly, it would increase the DGs' accountability for the overall quality of their impact assessments. Finally, it would save on administration costs, by avoiding the introduction of another procedural step between DGs and the CC.

Another available option that may increase the consistency of proposed regulations with the competitiveness goal is to involve competition authorities in the overall process when necessary. Much of the competitiveness principle is rooted in the elimination of obstacles to competition in specific markets, and the involvement of competition authorities at least in the consultation stage would guarantee that proposals do not place excessive burdens on firms' strategies, harming competition and consumer welfare. One easy way to involve competition policy-makers in the regulatory process is to publish the proposal on the competition authority's website for comments, as was proposed in Ireland during a recent consultation on better regulation.[271] A greater involvement of DG COMP with increased power to signal proposals that allegedly reduce the degree of competitiveness of individual relevant markets seems to be attracting growing interest among practioners and policy-makers.

An example of competitiveness-proofing that can be considered as embedded in the IA model is provided by the UK Office of Fair Trade's Competition Filter test, illustrated in Box 3. The competition assessment introduced in the UK in 2001 provides a very good example of how competitiveness issues (and competition authorities) can be involved in the

---

[271] See *Reports on submissions received arising from public consultation on Towards Better Regulation*, Department of the Taoiseach, December 2002, p. 9 ("Enterprise Energy Ireland proposes that a mechanism for proofing regulations from a competition perspective might be for the Competition Authority to publish proposed regulations on its website for a 14 day public consultation period. During this period any anti-competitive elements of the regulation for the relevant sector could be highlighted to the Authority. All sectors would thereby be provided with an opportunity to comment on legislation in advance of its implementation and such a process would also enhance the understanding of the Competition Authority of the different barriers to competition arising in various sectors").

RIA process. Table 9 lists the introduction of competition assessment as one of the suggestions for improving the competitiveness-proofing of ExIAs completed by lead DGs.

Box 3. The OFT's competition filter test

Following the Government's 2001 White Paper on Enterprise, Skills and Innovation, entitled *Opportunity for All in a World of Change,* a Regulatory Impact Assessment of proposed regulations is now required to include the identification and assessment of potential competition concerns or benefits.[272] For this reason, the Office of Fair Trade has published *ad hoc* guidelines for policy-makers in government departments who are in charge of performing regulatory impact assessment.[273] The UK Better Regulation Executive has also included a section on competition assessment on its website.[274] Under the new screen test, officials in charge of RIA have to perform an initial 'competition filter test', by answering the following nine questions:

1. *In the market(s) affected by the new regulation, does any firm have more than 10 per cent market share?*

2. *In the market(s) affected by the new regulation, does any firm have more than 20 per cent market share?*

3. *In the market(s) affected by the new regulation, do the largest three firms together have at least 50 per cent market share?*

4. *Would the costs of regulation affect some firms substantially more than others?*

5. *Is the regulation likely to affect the market structure, changing the number and size of firms?*

6. *Would the regulation lead to higher set-up costs for new or potential firms that existing firms do not have to meet?*

7. *Would the regulation lead to higher ongoing costs for new or potential firms that existing firms do not have to meet?*

8. *Is the sector characterised by rapid technological change?*

9. *Would the regulation restrict the ability of firms to choose the price, quality, range or location of their products?*

---

[272] The White Paper is available at *http://www.dti.gov.uk/opportunityforall/* (visited 5 December 2005).

[273] See Office of Fair Trade, *Guidelines for Competition Assessment –A guide for policymakers completing regulatory impact assessments,* OFT355, February 2002.

[274] See *www.cabinetoffice.gov.uk/regulation/ria/ria_guidance/competition_assessment.asp* (accessed 5 December 2005).

This implies that competent officials are required to engage in a market definition exercise, just as normally performed by competition authorities. Where there are more 'no' than 'yes' answers to the filter questions, the administration can conclude that the proposal is not likely to exert a significant impact on competition in the relevant market(s). In this case, the results of the filter test must be reported in the initial RIA form, and no further analysis of competition effects is carried out. Nonetheless, the initial RIA should carry a definition of the affected markets, a summary of the characteristics of each relevant market, and – most notably - a "clear statement about the anticipated positive and negative effects on competition for each policy option with an explanation of the reasoning behind the answers to the nine questions."[275]

Conversely, whenever there are more 'yes' answers than 'no', a 'detailed competition assessment' has to be included in the RIA. Such an assessment is very similar to that performed by competition authorities in scrutinising the prospective effects of mergers. It requires the sponsoring administration to consider all possible effects of a regulation, including any knock-on effects on related sectors; check whether these effects do in fact raise concerns for competition; and compare policy options in terms of their impact on competition, and, if possible, identify suitable alternative policy options. The detailed competition assessment is articulated in three steps: i) identifying directly and indirectly affected markets; ii) *understanding the current nature of competition*, by exploring supply and demand factors, market outcomes and the competitive process, and iii) *identifying the impacts of the regulation*, which mandatorily include both the direct and indirect impacts on competition resulting from each policy option presented in the RIA.

In performing the detailed competition assessment, sponsoring administrations can rely on an *ad hoc* structure at the Office of Fair Trade, called Regulatory Review Team.

Table 9. Recommendations on Roadmap 9 – Competitiveness-proofing

9.1 Include competitiveness in the IIA standard model by issuing guidelines on how to perform competitiveness-proofing or competition assessment.
9.2 Involve CC at the interim stage between the preliminary IA and the ExIA.
9.3 Allow the CC to signal ExIAs that do not sufficiently address competitiveness.
9.4 Involve DG COMP in the consultation process.
9.5 Introduce a competition filter test supported by the DG COMP.

---

[275] Ibid.

3.9   Roadmap 10 – Create a regulatory watchdog

Most of the roadmaps illustrated in previous sections crucially depend on the appointment of a centralised unit in charge of overseeing the implementation of the IIA model. The main problem in the EU is certainly not the absence of entities with expertise on impact assessment; on the contrary, it is the proliferation of administrative bodies linked to the Commission, the Council and the Parliament, each with autonomous activities in the field of better regulation and impact assessment.[276] As a matter of fact, none of these structures – and certainly not their sum – would be able to replicate the oversight functions performed by successfully created governmental and independent bodies in most OECD countries where impact assessment has produced some encouraging results. The absence of a dedicated, individual oversight body is certainly one of the evident limits of the current IIA model.

The need for an independent agency in charge of overseeing the implementation of the impact assessment procedure had been stressed even before the introduction of the IIA model in the EU. In the Final Report on the BIA system, the Commission stated that "weaknesses identified in the BIA system, particularly as regards the identification of proposals that should be subject to BIA and the quality check on the analysis carried out, indicate that a dedicated structure is needed to support an impact assessment process. This is also in accordance with international practice."[277] The Commission also acknowledged that such a structure should be given a mandate for issuing guidance and checking that the quality of the analysis is satisfactory, and suggested that "[p]referably, it should be situated centrally within the Commission in order to ensure transparency and coordination".[278]

This suggestion, however, was not transposed into the new IIA model introduced in 2003. Today, most of the problems encountered in the IIA experimental phase should 'ring a bell' in Brussels, and lead to a decision to remedy the 'original sin' of not appointing a supervising agency for what now appears as a quite uncoordinated and unsupervised assessment exercise.

---

[276] See European Commission Working Document, *Who is doing what on Better Regulation at EU Level – Organisation Charts*, op. cit.

[277] See the Commission's BIA Final Report, op. cit.

[278] Ibid.

The creation of (more than) one oversight body was already the subject of the so-called 'Doorn motion' at the European Parliament, as described above, in section 2.3. The model proposed by Doorn served exactly the purpose of reconciling the need for independent evaluation by DGs, the Council and the Parliament with the need to have an external agent overseeing the procedure, consulting with proposing administrations and highlighting significant inconsistencies and/or methodological flaws in the analysis. However, as already recalled, the model proposed would probably prove too complex and burdensome for EU administrations, which are currently feeling a strong urge to cut red tape and simplify administrative procedures. Endorsing such a three-tiered approach would, in addition, significantly jeopardise the convergence of approaches adopted by different EU institutions, thus increasing the likelihood of inconsistencies between adopted procedures and – from a more game-theoretical perspective – putting incentives on individual audits to behave strategically and compete against each other, in order to both legitimise their existence and serve the mandate of their principal institution. All these would translate into an increase, not a reduction, of administrative costs.

A more effective, cost-reducing and organisationally efficient model would entail the creation of a centralised agency for integrated impact assessment. As both Commission proposals and Council and Parliament amendments will be subjected to the IIA, a single task force is more likely to effectively guarantee the convergence of the assessment methods applied and avoid duplication in consultations and in competitiveness-proofing as well as in the assessments of subsidiarity, proportionality, cost-effectiveness, environmental and social impacts. A single clearinghouse for EU assessment exercises would also facilitate lesson-drawing and the identification of best practices.

Further support to the creation of dedicated oversight bodies for impact assessment carried out by proponent administrations comes from the OECD's extensive experience in surveying better regulation initiatives in developed countries. Since the late 1990s, OECD reports have always stated the importance of linking impact assessment to an oversight body as a key enabler of the success of regulatory impact analysis models.[279] Most

---

[279] Amongst the many OECD publications on this issue, see in particular *Designing Independent and Accountable Regulatory Authorities for High-Quality Regulation*, proceedings of the OECD Working Party on Regulatory Management and Reform,

recently, Josef Konvitz recalled that "[t]he relationship between an effective, comprehensive regulatory policy and the existence of a central oversight body appears to be strong. They are mutually supportive, and where one exists, the other is usually also present." Konvitz also highlighted that oversight bodies "can perform a number of different functions ... an advocacy role, a challenge function (the critical assessment of RIA), and practical and technical support for the application of regulatory tools". As a result, "[r]esources must be allocated to promote regulatory policy, for example to central oversight bodies, which need adequate authority for their tasks such as the formal oversight of RIA. Measures including sanctions must be built in to ensure compliance with regulatory quality processes and tools."[280]

Moreover, authoritative scholars such as Robert Hahn and Robert Litan have recently advocated the creation of a "strong centralised oversight unit to help evaluate significant regulatory proposals" at EU level, adding that "states that do not have such unit should consider creating them".[281] Hahn and Litan also specified that the centralised unit should have a status similar to the units it will have to discipline (i.e. lead DGs); that the unit should take on a leadership role in establishing information quality and regulatory guidelines both for EU and member state policy-makers; that the unit should be given the power to challenge proposals that do not carry a sufficient or satisfactory estimate of net benefits; that it should publish its findings on the Internet; that it should publish a comprehensive annual report on the costs and benefits of EU regulation; and that it should be adequately funded in order to provide training for EU regulators and better information to MEPs.[282]

Finally, most scholarly literature considers the delegation of policy-making powers to regulatory agencies as a solution that maximises regulatory legitimacy and credibility. Enhancing the credibility of the EU

London, 10-11 January 2005 (available at *http://www.oecd.org/dataoecd/15/28/35028836.pdf* – accessed 5 December 2005).

[280] See J. Konvitz, "The Institutional Context for Better Regulation", paper presented at the Conference on Simple is Better: Effective Regulation for a More Competitive Europe, Amsterdam, 7-8 October 2004, p. 8.

[281] See Hahn and Litan, op. cit., p. 503. See also C. Radaelli, "The Diffusion of Regulatory Impact Analysis in OECD Countries: Best Practices or Lesson-Drawing?", *European Journal of Political Research*, 43(5), 2004, pp. 723-747.

[282] See Hahn and Litan, op. cit., p. 503.

IIA model has been recently defined as an overarching goal for EU institutions, even with respect to other priorities, such as efficient regulation.[283] Well-known scholars have also advocated the creation of agencies whenever the regulatory issues to be tackled exhibit increased technical and scientific complexity, as is the case for the IIA exercise.[284] Other commentators have argued that the creation of *ad hoc* regulatory agencies can facilitate the involvement of certain groups in the decision-making process.[285] And some have argued that a centralised regulatory agency could profit from scale economies, collecting experience and expertise and emerging as a one-stop-shop also for member state administrations in charge of impact assessment.[286]

In summary, a widespread consensus seems to be emerging on the merit of creating a centralised regulatory oversight unit for EU impact assessment, with enhanced advocacy, consulting, oversight and challenge functions. However, the road to achieving such goal is punctuated by a number of question marks, concerning in particular: i) the governance structure of the unit; ii) the powers and the functions it should be granted; iii) the expertise it should collect; and iv) the timing and scope of its intervention.

As regards the governance structure of the oversight body, several alternative options should be considered. First, the governmental or non-governmental nature of the unit should be addressed. Examples of governmental bodies performing oversight functions in OECD countries

---

[283] See C. Radaelli, *What Does Regulatory Impact Assessment Mean in Europe?*, op. cit., p. 20 ("the lesson to learn about the diffusion of impact assessment is that legitimacy is much more important than efficiency. The two are intertwined, of course, as an efficient RIA is more credible than wrong economic analysis of regulatory proposals. But the point is that credibility is the Achilles' heel of impact assessment").

[284] See R. Baldwin and C. McCrudden, *Regulation and Public Law*, London: Weidenfeld and Nicolson, 1987, p. 4.

[285] See M. Everson, G. Majone, L. Metcalfe and A. Schout, *The Role of Specialised Agencies in Decentralising EU Governance*, Report to the Commission, 1999 (available at *http://europa.eu.int/comm/governance/areas/group6/index_en.htm* – visited 5 December 2005); and D. Geradin, *The Development of European Regulatory Agencies: What the EU should Learn from the American Experience*, forthcoming on the Columbia Journal of European Law, 2005.

[286] See Hahn and Litan, op. cit., p. 494.

include the OIRA in the US and the BRE in the UK, whereas other countries, such as Sweden, Denmark, the Netherlands, Japan and Mexico, have created non-governmental bodies reporting directly to the Parliament. Australia is probably the most extreme case. The State of Victoria allows any competent person or organisation to certify that a RIA document complies with the relevant requirements.[287] As a result, even external scholars are allowed to perform the challenge function normally attributed to institutional oversight bodies.

The EU case, however, is certainly peculiar in this respect. In the IIA model, oversight would be needed on all regulatory proposals subjected to extended impact assessment, which include major Commission initiatives and amendments proposed by the Council and the Parliament under the co-decision procedure. Against this backdrop, the available options for the creation of an oversight agency would include: establishing an independent monitoring agency; an inter-institutional agency; a unit rooted in the Commission's Secretariat-General; or an agency dependent on the Competitiveness Council or one of the Parliament's Committees.[288]

From a theoretical standpoint, none of the above-mentioned options strictly dominates the others. Furthermore, the EU's peculiar institutional setting needs to be taken into due account before deciding on the governance structure to be given to the new regulatory unit. As a matter of fact, the EU model of policy initiation and formulation has significantly departed from the traditional 'separation of powers' by establishing an indigenous "institutional balance of powers" approach, deeply rooted in the principle of 'non-interference' introduced from the outset in Article 4 of the Treaty of Rome. According to such principle, each EU institution must strictly adhere to the limits of the individual competences assigned to it by the Treaty.[289] Within this wider framework, the EU institutions have developed their own model of policy-making, which almost fully delegates policy initiation powers to the Commission. For such reason, creating an inter-institutional unit to oversee and challenge impact assessments performed by individual DGs would at least seem hazardous – and

---

[287] See the *Subordinate Legislation Act 1994* (available at *http://www.dms.dpc.vic.gov.au/* visited 5 December 2005).

[288] See OECD, *Regulatory Performance: Ex Post Evaluation of Regulatory Tools and Institutions*, op. cit., pp. 15-19, for a taxonomy and overall assessment of governance structures.

[289] See e.g. Everson, Majone, Metcalfe and Schout, op. cit., p. 27.

evidence confirms that no similar structure exists in the EU. Furthermore, the Inter-institutional Agreement on Better Law-Making signed in 2003 specifies that the Commission should keep taking the lead on impact assessment, and ensure that the result of its activities is made available to the Council and the Parliament.[290] The two most viable options would therefore be the creation of an independent oversight agency and the creation of a specialised unit within the Commission's Secretariat-General.[291]

The identification of the best option would inevitably depend on the choice of the powers and duties that the oversight agency should be granted. The more extensive and far-reaching such powers and duties are, the less likely that an independent agency can be called upon to perform them. These would inevitably include advocacy, consulting, guidance, challenge, coordination of existing initiatives, training, yearly reporting and keeping institutional relations. Table 10 describes in more detail the powers and duties a centralised regulatory unit should have in order to effectively oversee the implementation of the IIA model.

Table 10. Powers and duties of an ideal centralised regulatory unit for IIA

Powers/Duties	Description	Timing
Advocacy	- Participate in the advocacy process by identifying areas in which regulatory reform would be needed, with specific emphasis on areas in which administrative burdens appear excessive and SMEs are faced with overwhelming red tape - Issue 'prompt letters' by suggesting initiatives by individual DGs in identified areas of regulatory reform	Ongoing

---

[290] See European Parliament, Report on the Commission White Paper on European Governance, op. cit.

[291] An alternative would be the creation of two groups, as in the UK. There, the BRE (formerly named RIU) acts as a centralised regulatory oversight unit, but also hosts the BRTF, an independent group in charge of monitoring the compliance of RIAs with the principles of good regulation. See, inter alia, OECD, *Designing Independent and Accountable Regulatory Authorities for High-Quality Regulation*, op. cit., p. 49.

	- Issue suggestions on the choice of regulatory options to be considered, by promoting the assessment of self-regulatory and other 'light touch' options - Gather opinions from stakeholders on areas in which regulatory costs are excessive and submit them to individual DGs	
Consulting	- Provide assistance to DGs at an early stage of drafting the preliminary and extended impact assessment forms - Intervene in early drafts by suggesting more in-depth assessment of compliance with competitiveness, subsidiarity, proportionality, reduction of administrative burdens requirements, etc. - Help DGs in performing competition assessments - Help Council and Parliament in assessing the impact of major amendments to Commission proposals	Ongoing
Guidance	- Issue guidelines on methodological issues, such as testing the compliance with competitiveness, subsidiarity, proportionality, reduction of administrative burdens requirements, etc. - Issue guidelines on competition assessment - Collaborate with individual DGs in defining sector-specific impact assessment methodologies and in their periodical reviews	Periodical
Challenge	- Power to reject proposals not accompanied by a satisfactory impact assessment form - Power to impose the drafting of an ExIA if the agency has performed only a preliminary IA - Power to impose amendments in terms of more extensive stakeholder consultation, screening for administrative costs, proportionality, subsidiarity, competitiveness, etc.	When needed

	- Power to impose a competition assessment - Power to impose the calculation of net benefits	
Coordination	- Coordination of the relaunched IIA model with existing initiatives/pilot projects at EU level, such as BEST, SLIM, IRQ, etc. - Coordination with DG COMP for performance of competition assessments - Coordination with existing groups active in the field of better regulation, such as the DEBR, the High Level Group, Council and Parliament *ad hoc* groups, etc. - Coordination with national units responsible for impact assessment	Ongoing
Training	- Organise training sessions for EU public officials, involving also practitioners and academicians - Provide training to officials responsible for impact assessment in individual member states	Ongoing
Reporting	- Publish yearly reports on the net benefits of major EU legislation - Publish the results of oversight activities on the Internet - Report to the Competitiveness Council on simplification priorities and competition assessments performed	Yearly
Institutional relations	- Report to meetings of the Competitiveness Council on simplification priorities and competition assessments performed - Report to Parliament on oversight activities carried out every year and on Parliament's request - Cooperate with the US Office of Management and Budget in the US-Commission Dialogue on regulatory and impact assessment practices launched in Washington, D.C. on 20 June 2005	Periodical

Turning to the issue of expertise, most functions embedded in the oversight body would certainly call for the appointment of specialised staff with extensive expertise in the field of economic, environmental and social impact assessment. The unit should be able to challenge proposed regulations both for the failure to comply with procedural steps as well as in cases where the substantive assessment is lacking methodological soundness. An issue that has been raised is whether the 'regulatory watchdog' should do the analysis itself or commission it to external experts, by engaging in spot or framework contracting with practitioners, consultants or academicians. From this perspective, a trade-off seems to emerge between the need to develop an independent expertise and the difficulty and costliness of creating a single unit with all the required expertise to scrutinise economic, social and environmental assessments performed by all DGs across widely disparate fields. A wise solution would consist in initially relying on external experts, and gradually requiring that the unit performs in-house analyses by drawing on past and consolidated experience.

Table 11. Recommendations on Roadmap 10 – Creating a regulatory watchdog

10.1 Create a centralised regulatory unit rooted in the Commission's Secretariat-General.

10.2 Empower the unit with roles of advocacy, consulting, guidance, challenge, coordination of existing initiatives, training, yearly reporting and keeping institutional relations.

10.3 Allow for initial reliance on external expertise, and gradual development of in-house knowledge and competences.

4. Conclusion: It's a long way to Lisbon

The importance of impact assessment as a key tool to ensure the viability of proposed pieces of legislation has been acknowledged by scholars of a significant number of disciplines in the social sciences. Mainstream economists consider impact assessment as a method to compare prospective direct and indirect costs and benefits of proposed regulations, and to assess the desirability of a given regulatory option by using some form of efficiency criterion, whether it be the Pareto or Kaldor-Hicks efficiency criterion, mixed tests accounting for justice or distributive issues such as the Kaldor-Hicks-Zerbe Jr. criterion, the recently proposed KHM criterion, the lexicographical criterion developed by John Rawls, or some other measure.[292]

Game theorists and scholars in the economic theory of organisation tend to consider impact assessment as an instrument of accountability, within a broader framework in which public administrations, legislative and government structures are analysed as a complex, multi-level nexus of principal-agent relationships. For example, distinguished scholars in law and economics have analysed CBA and RIA as tools to increase the principal's degree of control over bureaucrat-agents, a goal that is considered as *per se* more important than the actual scientific soundness of the assessment exercise.[293]

---

[292] For an overview of most criteria, see F. Parisi and J. Klick, "Functional Law and Economics: The Search for Value-Neutral Principles of Lawmaking", *Chicago-Kent Law Review*, 79, 2004, pp. 431-450; but also J.R. Hicks, "The Foundations of Welfare Economics", *Economic Journal*, 49, 1939, pp. 696-712; N. Kaldor, "Welfare Propositions of Economics and Inter-personal Comparisons of Utility", *Economic Journal*, 49, 1939, pp. 549-52; R.O. Zerbe Jr., "Is Cost-Benefit Analysis Legal? Three Rules", *Journal of Policy Analysis and Management*, 17, 1998, pp. 419-456; and R.O. Zerbe Jr., Y. Bauman and A. Finkle, *An Aggregate Measure for Benefit-Cost Analysis*, Working Paper 05-13, AEI-Brookings Joint Centre for Regulatory Studies, Washington, D.C., August 2005.

[293] See E.A. Posner, *Controlling Agencies*, op. cit.

More generally, economic theory suggests that, when using *ex ante* policy evaluation tools, the absolute outcome of the evaluation is less important than the relative, comparative result – i.e. RIA becomes useful when it provides support in deciding which regulatory option should be undertaken, by enabling the use of criteria and tests that exert a neutral impact on all the regulatory options to be compared. Such an agnostic view of RIA, of course, highlights the importance of using quali-quantitative tools at an early stage, before the regulatory option has been chosen.

Lawyers, on the other hand, tend to see impact assessment as a standardised procedure that legitimises and integrates the choice to delegate powers to dependent and independent administrations. The distinction between pro-forma RIA, informative RIA and integrated RIA developed by the UK National Audit Office is useful in this respect.[294] In the first case, RIA becomes a procedural requirement that integrates and standardises the regulatory process, and only helps governments and parliaments in observing the underlying rationale that led an individual department or agency to undertake a given policy option. In the second case, RIA can be used as a communication tool, for example, in a late consultation process or in implementing the regulatory option, thus mostly to increase transparency vis-à-vis targeted groups. Whereas only in the third case, the results of impact assessment exert a significant impact on the policy option chosen by proposing administrations. Thus, from a lawyer's perspective, the timing, scope and procedural aspects of a RIA are the most important and decisive: failure to complete a RIA form should lead to sanctions by competent administrations, and to the consequent annulment of regulations not backed by a sufficiently exhaustive RIA.

Finally, political scientists tend to award priority to the contextual dimension of impact assessment. As has been recently stated, depending on the institutional context in which it is introduced, RIA can become a way to coordinate policy, an expression of formal bureaucratic behaviour, an efficiency-oriented set of tests or a creature geared towards enabling a common discourse in a world dominated by multi-level, disintegrated governance. In the EU case, failure to provide RIA with a specific identity and function has been considered as a typical way to "disguise political-distributional problems under the veil of pseudo-methodological problems".[295]

---

[294] See e.g. The *Compendium Report 2004-2005*, op. cit., p. 3.

[295] Radaelli, *What does Regulatory Impact Assessment Mean in Europe?*, op. cit., p. 11.

In this paper, I tried to take into account all the abovementioned perspectives by presenting an integrated, interdisciplinary discussion of the most urgent issues that may be addressed in the review of the EU integrated Impact Assessment model, scheduled for early 2006. Far from representing a complete picture, this analysis is conceived for policy-makers as possible 'food for thought' in discussing the upcoming review.

The main conclusion that can be drawn from the present analysis is clear. On the one hand, EU institutions are relying heavily on impact assessment as a shortcut to Lisbon. And in doing so, they are announcing future savings in business compliance costs and in administrative costs, a yet-unknown pervasiveness of cost-benefit analyses, a higher level of coordination between EU institutions, and finally a more transparent, accountable, 'open' regulatory process to the benefit of next generation businesses and citizens.[296] On the other hand, however, the results achieved so far in this direction are, to say the least, poor. Before the gap gets too wide, the Commission, the Council and the Parliament should take action to take the review of the IIA model seriously.

Evidence from other international experiences as well as from the past EU experience reveal that it is preferable not to have RIA, than to have a bad one. And EU institutions, especially after the French and Dutch 'no' votes on the European Constitution and the latest disappointing economic results, cannot count on the power of the gospel. If the Commission really has the numbers, then action must be taken seriously and now to increase the methodological soundness, transparency, cost-effectiveness and external oversight of impact assessments. And similar procedures must be included in national Lisbon strategies. For these reasons, the upcoming review of the impact assessment model, expected in early 2006, is even more crucial than it might *prima facie* seem. If Europe fails to square the circle, the panacea is likely to become a Pandora's box, leading, on the one hand, to fertile ground for regulatory capture; on the other, to more 'scientific' attempts to defend the virtues of vicious pieces of legislation. In other words, a scapegoat both for the regulators and for the regulated.

---

[296] On the concept of 'openness' in regulatory processes, see OECD, *Modernising Government: The Way Forward*, op. cit.

SELECTED REFERENCES

Academic Literature

Ackerman, F. and L. Heinzerling, *Priceless: On Knowing the Price of Everything and the Value of Nothing*, New York: The New Press, 2004.

Ackerman, F., L. Heinzerling and R. Massey, *Applying Cost-Benefit to Past Decisions: Was environmental protection ever a good idea?*, Georgetown Public Law Research Paper No. 576161, Georgetown University, August 2004.

Adler, M.D. and E.A. Posner, *Cost-Benefit Analysis: Legal, Economic, and Philosophical Perspectives*, Chicago, IL: University of Chicago Press, 2001.

Arculus, D., speech to the staff of the Financial Services Authority, 29 June 2005 (available at *http://www.fsa.gov.uk/Pages/Library/Communication/Speeches/2005/0705_sda.shtml*).

Arrow, K., et al., *Benefit-Cost Analysis in Environmental, Health, and Safety Regulation: A Statement of Principles*, AEI/Brookings Joint Center for Regulatory Studies, Washington, D.C., 1996 (available at *http://aei-brookings.org/publications/books/benefit_cost_analysis.pdf*).

Baldwin, R. and C. McCrudden, *Regulation and Public Law*, London: Weidenfeld and Nicolson, 1987.

Boardman, A.E., *Cost-benefit Analysis: Concepts and Practice*, Upper Saddle River, NJ: Prentice Hall, 1997.

Boden R., J. Froud, A. Ogus and P. Stubbs, *Controlling the Regulators*, London: MacMillan Press, 1998.

Bosanquet, N., "Sir Keith's Reading List", *Political Quarterly*, 52(3), pp. 324-341, 1983.

Breyer, S., "Regulation and Deregulation in the United States", in G. Majone (ed.), *De-regulation or Re-regulation? Regulatory Reform in Europe and the United States*, London: Pinter Publishers, 1990.

COSAC (Conference of Community and European Affairs Committees of Parliaments of the European Union), *Report on developments in European Union procedures and practices relevant to parliamentary scrutiny*, 30 April 2004.

Craswell, R., "Passing on the Costs of Legal Rules: Efficiency and Distribution in Buyer-Seller Relationships", *Stanford Law Review*, Vol. 43, 1991.

Donev, G., "Methodology for Regulatory Impact Assessment Related to Occupational Safety and Health", paper presented at the International Seminar on Implementation of Regulatory Impact Assessment: Best Practices in Europe, AUBG, Blagoevgrad, Bulgaria, 8-11 June 2004.

Driesen, D., *Is Cost-Benefit Analysis Neutral?*, 2 February 2005 (available at *http://ssrn.com/abstract=663602*).

Everson, M., G. Majone, L. Metcalfe and A. Schout, *The Role of Specialised Agencies in Decentralising EU Governance*, Report to the Commission, 1999 (available at *http://europa.eu.int/comm/governance/areas/group6/index_en.htm*).

Friedman, B.D., *Regulation in the Reagan-Bush Era: The Eruption of Presidential Influence*, Pittsburgh, PA: Pittsburgh University Press, 1995.

Frontier Economics, *Wrong Numbers – Difficulties in Estimating the Welfare Gains from Regulation*, Bulletin, June 2005.

Gaebler, T., J. Blackman, L. Blessing, R. Bruce, W. Keene and P. Smith, *Positive Outcomes: Raising the Bar on Government Reinvention*, Burke, VA: Chatelaine Press, 1999.

Gattuso, J.L., *What is the Bush Administration's Record on Regulatory Reform?*, testimony before the Subcommittee on Energy Policy, Natural Resources and Regulatory Affairs Committee on Government Reform, US House of Representatives, 17 November 2004 (available at *http://www.heritage.org/Research/Regulation/tst111604a.cfm* – visited 1 August 2005).

Geradin, D., *The Development of European Regulatory Agencies: What the EU should Learn from the American Experience*, forthcoming on the Columbia Journal of European Law, 2005 (available at *http://www.ieje.net/fileadmin/IEJE/Pdf/European_regulatory_agencies.pdf*)

Gore, Alfred, *From Red Tape to Results: Creating a Government that Works Better and Costs Less*, Report of the National Performance Review (US Government body), 1993.

Hagerup, B., "Business Impact Assessment – The Danish Model", paper presented at the Seminar on Regulatory Transparency: The Use of Public Consultation to Improve the Investment Climate, Thessaloniki, Greece, 22-23 November 2002 (available at *http://www.oecd.org/dataoecd/58/39/2410437.pdf*).

Hahn, R.W., *Regulatory Reform: Assessing the Government's Numbers*, AEI-Brookings Center for Regulatory Studies, Working Paper No. 99-06, Washington, D.C., 1999.

--------, *In Defense of the Economic Analysis of Regulation*, American Enterprise Institute, Washington, D.C., 2005.

Hahn, R.W. and R. Litan, *An Analysis of the Third Government Report on the Benefits and Costs of Federal Regulation*, AEI-Brookings Joint Center for Regulatory Studies, Washington, D.C., 2000.

Hahn, R.W., J. Burnett, Chan Yee-Ho, E. Mader and P. Moyle, "Assessing Regulatory Impact Analysis: The Failure of Agencies to Comply with Executive Order 12866", *Harvard Journal of Law and Policy*, Vol. 23, No. 3, 2000.

Hahn, R.W. and Cass R. Sunstein, *Regulatory Oversight Takes Exciting New Tack*, Working Paper No. 01-25, AEI-Brookings Joint Center for Regulatory Studies, Washington, D.C., 2001.

Hahn, R. and C. Sunstein, "New Executive Order for Improving Federal Regulation? Deeper and Wider Cost-Benefit Analysis", *University of Pennsylvania Law Review*, Vol. 150, No. 1489, 2002.

Hahn, R.W. and M.B. Muething, "The Grand Experiment in Regulatory Reporting", *Administrative Law Review*, Vol. 55, No. 3, 2003, pp. 607-642.

Hahn, R. and P. Dudley, *How well does the Government do cost-benefit analysis?*, Working Paper 04-01, AEI-Brookings Joint Center for Regulatory Studies, Washington, D.C., 2004.

Hahn, R.W. and R.E. Litan, "Counting Regulatory Benefits and Costs: Lessons for the U.S. and Europe", *Journal of International Economic Law*, Vol. 8, No. 2, 2005, pp. 473-508.

Hampton, P., *Reducing Administrative Burdens: Effective Inspection and Enforcement*, 2004 (available at *http://www.hm-treasury.gov.uk/media/935/ 64/Hampton_Interim_Report_ 709.pdf*).

Harrington, W., "RIA Assessment Methods", paper prepared for the OECD project on *ex post* evaluation of regulatory tools and institutions, OECD, Paris, 2004.

Harrington, W. and R.D. Morgenstern, "Evaluating Regulatory Impact Analyses", paper prepared for the OECD project on *ex post* evaluation of regulatory tools and institutions, OECD, Paris, 2003.

Hicks, J.R., "The Foundations of Welfare Economics", *Economic Journal*, Vol. 49, 1939, pp. 696-712.

Kaldor, N., "Welfare Propositions of Economics and Inter-personal Comparisons of Utility", *Economic Journal*, Vol. 49, 1939, pp. 549-552.

Kamensky, J., "The US Reform Experience: The National Performance Review", paper presented at the Conference on Civil Service Systems in Comparative Perspectives, Indiana University, Bloomington, IN, 6 April

1997 (available from the US Government archive at *http://govinfo.library.unt.edu/npr/library/papers/bkgrd/kamensky.html*).

Kleinertova, J., "Specifics and Problems of RIA in Transition Economics and How to Overcome Them", paper presented at the International Seminar on Implementation of Regulatory Impact Assessment: Best Practices in Europe, AUBG, Blagoevgrad, Bulgaria, 8-11 June 2004.

Konvitz, J., "The Institutional Context for Better Regulation", paper presented at the Conference on Simple is Better: Effective Regulation for a More Competitive Europe, Amsterdam, 7-8 October 2004.

KPMG, *The CEO's Guide to International Business Costs*, 2004.

Laffont, J.J. and D. Martimort, *The Theory of Incentives: The Principal-Agent Model*, Princeton, NJ: Princeton University Press, 2002.

Lane, J.E., *New Public Management*, London: Routledge, 2000.

Lazer, D., "Regulatory Review: Presidential Control through Selective Communication and Institutionalized Conflict", 1998 (available at *http://www.ksg.harvard.edu/prg/lazer/control.pdf*).

Lee, N. and C. Kirkpatrick, *A Pilot Study of the Quality of European Commission Extended Impact Assessments*, IARC Working Paper Series No. 8, Impact Assessment Research Centre, University of Manchester, 2004 (available at *http://idpm.man.ac.uk/iarc/Reports/IARCWP8.DOC.pdf*).

Lussis, B., *EU Extended Impact Assessment Review*, Institut pour un Développement Durable Working Paper, 9 December 2004 (available at *http://users.skynet.be/idd/documents/EIDDD/WP01.pdf*).

Lutter, R., *Economic Analysis of Regulation in the U.S.: What Lessons for the European Commission?*, AEI-Brookings Joint Center for Regulatory Studies, Washington, D.C., 2001.

McGarity, T.O., "Regulatory Analysis and Regulatory Reform", *Texas Law Review*, Vol. 65, No. 1243, 1987.

Moe, T., "Regulatory performance and presidential administration", *American Journal of Political Science*, 26(2), 1982, pp. 197-224.

--------, "Control and feedback in economic regulation: The case of the NLRB", *American Political Science Review*, 79, 1985, pp. 1094-1016.

--------, "The new economics of organization", *American Journal of Political Science*, 1979, pp. 1094-1117.

Morgenstern, R.D., *Economic Analyses at EPA: Assessing Regulatory Impact*, Resources for the Future, Washington, D.C., 1997.

Morrall III, J., "An Assessment of the U.S. Regulatory Impact Assessment Program", in *Regulatory Impact Analysis: Best Practices in the Main OECD Countries*, OECD, Paris, 1997.

--------, "Ebbs and Flows in the Quality of Regulatory Analysis", speech at the Weidenbaum Center Forum on Executive Regulatory Analysis: Surveying the record, making it work, National Press Club, Washington, D.C., 17 December 2001 (available at *http://wc.wustl.edu/ ExecutiveRegulatoryReviewTranscripts/Morrall.pdf*).

Morrison, A., "OMB Interference with Agency Rulemaking: The Wrong Way to Write a Regulation", *Harvard Law Review*, Vol. 99, No. 1059, 1986.

Munger, M., *Analyzing Policy: Choices, Conflicts and Practices*, New York, NY: W.W. Norton & Co., 2000.

Munnich, N., *The Regulatory Burdens and Administrative Compliance Costs for Companies*, survey by the Confederation of Swedish Enterprise, Brussels Office, 2004.

Niskanen, W.A., *Bureaucracy and Representative Government*, Chicago, IL: Aldine, 2001.

--------, "The Weak Fourth Leg of Reaganomics", *Wall Street Journal*, 30 June 1988.

OECD (Organisation for Economic Cooperation and Development), *Regulatory Impact Analysis: Best Practice in OECD Countries*, Paris, 1997.

--------, *Regulatory Reform in the United States: Government Capacity to Ensure High-Quality Regulation*, Paris, 1999.

--------, *The OECD Review of Regulatory Reform in the United States*, Paris, 1999.

--------, *From Red Tape to Smart Tape: Administrative Simplification in OECD Countries*, Paris, 2003.

--------, "Regulatory Impact Analysis (RIA) Inventory", note by the Secretariat, 29th Session of the OECD Public Governance Committee, International Energy Agency, Paris, 2004.

--------, *Regulatory Performance: Ex-Post Evaluation of Regulatory Tools and Institutions*, Paris, 2004.

--------, *Economic Survey of the United Kingdom*, Paris, 2004.

--------, *Modernising Government: The Way Forward*, Paris, 2005.

--------, "Designing Independent and Accountable Regulatory Authorities for High-Quality Regulation", proceedings of the OECD Working Party on Regulatory Management and Reform, London, 10-11 January 2005 (available at *http://www.oecd.org/dataoecd/15/28/35028836.pdf*).

Opoku, C. and A. Jordan, "Impact Assessment in the EU: A Global Sustainable Development Perspective", paper presented at the Berlin Conference on the Human Dimension of Global Environmental Change, 3-4 December 2004 (available at *http://www.fu-berlin.de/ffu/akumwelt/bc2004/download/opoku_jordan_f.pdf* – visited 3 August 2005).

Osborne, D. and T. Gaebler, *Reinventing Government: How the Entrepreneurial Spirit is Transforming the Public Sector*, New York, NY: Addison-Wesley Publishing Co., 1992.

Parisi, F. and J. Klick, "Functional Law and Economics: The Search for Value-Neutral Principles of Lawmaking", *Chicago-Kent Law Review*, 79, 2004, pp. 431-450.

Parker, R., "Grading the Government", *University of Chicago Law Review*, 70, 2003.

Pelkmans, J., S. Labory and G. Majone, "Better EU Regulatory Quality: Assessing Current Initiatives and New Proposals", in G. Galli and J. Pelkmans (eds), *Regulatory Reform and Competitiveness in Europe*, Cheltenham: Edward Elgar, Vol. 1, 2000.

Pierce, M., *Computer-based models in integrated environmental assessment*, EEA Technical Report No. 14, European Energy Agency, 1999.

Pildes, R.H. and C.R. Sunstein, "Reinventing the Regulatory State", *University of Chicago Law Review*, Vol. 62, No. 1, 1995.

Pollitt, C. and G. Bouckaert, *Public Management Reform. A Comparative Analysis*, Oxford: Oxford University Press, 2000.

Posner, E.A., "Controlling Agencies with Cost-benefit Analysis: A Positive Political Theory Perspective", *University of Chicago Law Review*, Vol. 68, 2001.

--------, "Controlling Agencies with Cost-Benefit Analysis: A Positive Political Theory Perspective", *University of Chicago Law Review*, Vol. 68, No. 1137, 2001.

Radaelli, C., "The Diffusion of Regulatory Impact Analysis in OECD Countries: Best Practices or Lesson-drawing?", *European Journal of Political Research*, 43(5), 2004, pp. 723-747.

--------, "How Context Matters: Regulatory Quality in the European Union", paper prepared for the Special Issue on Policy Convergence of the *Journal of European Public Policy*, 2004.

--------, *What Does Regulatory Impact Assessment Mean in Europe?*, AEI-Brookings Joint Center for Regulatory Studies, Working Paper No. 05-02, Washington, D.C., January 2005.

Rajdlova, J., "Impact Assessment in a Country of Reforms – Slovak Experience", paper presented at the International Seminar on Implementation of Regulatory Impact Assessment: Best Practices in Europe, AUBG, Blagoevgrad, Bulgaria, 8-11 June 2004.

Rodriguez, L., "Constitutional and Statutory Limits for Cost-Benefit Analysis Pursuant to Executive Orders 12291 and 12498", *Environmental Affairs Law Review*, Vol. 15, No. 505, 1988.

Staronova, K., "Analysis of the Policy-Making Process in Slovakia", 2003 (available at *http://www.policy.hu/staronova/FinalResearch.pdf*).

Sunstein, C.R., *The Cost-Benefit State*, University of Chicago Law School, John M. Olin Law & Economics, Working Paper No. 39, May 1996.

Sunstein, C., *Risk and Reason. Safety, Law and the Environment*, Cambridge: Cambridge University Press, 2002.

Toth, F.L., *Participatory integrated assessment methods - An assessment of their usefulness to the European Environmental Agency*, EEA Technical Report No. 64, European Environment Agency, Copenhagen, 2001.

Van Den Bergh, R., "Towards Efficient Self-Regulation in Markets for Professional Services", 2005 (available at *http://www.hertig.ethz.ch/LE_2005_files/Papers*).

Vander Beken, T., "Legislative crime proofing - Detection and evaluation of loopholes that offer opportunities for organised crime", presentation at the first European Congress on developing public/private partnerships to reduce the harm of organised crime, Dublin, 21 November 2003 (available at *http://www.ircp.be/uploaded/dublin-21-11-2003.ppt*).

Vibert, F., *The EU's New System of Regulatory Impact Assessment – A Scorecard*, European Policy Forum, London, 2004.

Weidenbaum, M., *Regulatory Process Reform from Ford to Clinton*, CATO Institute, 2000 (available at *www.cato.org/pubs/regulation/reg20n1a.html*).

West, W.F., "The Institutionalization of Regulatory Review: Organizational Stability and Responsive Competence at OIRA", *Presidential Studies Quarterly*, No. 1, Center for the Study of the Presidency, 2005.

Woodward, B. and D.S. Broder, "Quayle's Quest: Curb Rules, Leave 'No Fingerprints'", *Washington Post*, 9 January 1992.

World Bank, *Doing Business in 2005: Understanding Regulation*, Washington, D.C., September 2004.

Zerbe, Jr., R.O., Y. Bauman and A. Finkle, *An Aggregate Measure for Benefit-Cost Analysis*, AEI-Brookings Joint Centre for Regulatory Studies, Working Paper 05-13, Washington, D.C., August 2005.

Zerbe, Jr., R.O., "Is Cost-Benefit Analysis Legal? Three Rules", *Journal of Policy Analysis and Management*, Vol. 17, 1998, pp. 419-456.

EU Materials

BEST, Report of the Business Environment Simplification Task Force, 1998 (available at *http://europa.eu.int/comm/enterprise/enterprise_policy/best*).

DEBR (ad hoc group of Directors and Experts on Better Regulation), *Report to the Ministers responsible for Public Administration in the EU member states on the progress of the implementation of the Mandelkern Report's Action Plan on Better Regulation*, Athens, 2003.

European Commission, Communication of 6 November 1996, COM(96)559 (Report of the Commission on the SLIM Pilot Project), 1996 (available at *http://europa.eu.int/comm/internal_market/simplification/docs/com1996-559/com1996-559_en.pdf*).

European Commission, White Paper on European Governance, COM(2001)727, 25 July 2001.

European Commission, Preparatory Work for the White Paper, 2002, p. 119.

European Commission, Action Plan on Simplifying and improving the regulatory environment (COM(2002) 278), 2002.

European Commission, Better regulation Action Plan, COM(2002)278, 5 June 2002.

European Commission, BIA Final Report, *Lessons Learned and the Way Forward*, Enterprise Paper No. 9, 2002 (available at *http://europa.eu.int/comm/enterprise/library/enterprise-papers/pdf/enterprise_paper_09_2002.pdf*).

European Commission, Communication from the Commission to the European parliament, the Council, the Economic and Social Committee and the Committee of the Regions, *Towards a Global Partnership for Sustainable Development*, COM(2002)82, 12 February 2002.

European Commission, Communication on better monitoring of the application of community law (COM(2002) 725), 2002.

European Commission, Communication on framework for target-based tripartite contracts (COM(2002) 709), 2002.

European Commission, Communication on general principles and minimum standards for consultation (COM(2002)704), 2002.

European Commission, Communication on impact assessment (COM(2002) 276), including internal *Guidelines*, 2002.

European Commission, Communication on operating framework for the European Regulatory Agencies (COM(2002) 718), 2002.

European Commission, Communication on proposal for a new comitology decision (COM(2002) 719), 2002.

European Commission, Communication on Simplifying and improving the regulatory environment (COM(2002) 278), 2002.

European Commission, Communication on the collection and use of expertise (COM(2002) 713), 2002.

European Commission, Staff Working Paper, *Impact Assessment: Next Steps - In Support of Competitiveness and Sustainable Development*, SEC(2004)1377, 2004.

European Commission, Working Document, *Who is doing what on Better Regulation at EU Level – Organisation Charts*, 1 July 2004 (available at *http://www.eipa.nl/Topics/EPMF/documents/EU_Who_is_who_Better_regulati on_July_04_sh_update.doc* – visited 4August 2005).

European Commission, *A Handbook for Impact Assessment in the Commission - How to do an Impact Assessment*, 2005.

European Commission, *Annual Evaluation Review 2004 – Overview of the Commission's Findings and Activities*, SEC(2005)587, 2005.

European Commission, Better Regulation for Growth and Jobs in the European Union, COM(2005)97, 16 March 2005.

European Commission, Communication to the Spring European Council on "Working together for Growth and Jobs – A New Start for the Lisbon Strategy", COM(2005)24, 2 February 2005.

European Commission, Enterprise DG, Final Report of the Pilot Project "Ex-Post Evaluation of EC Legislation and its Burden on Business", 2005.

European Commission, Impact Assessment Guidelines, SEC(2005)971, 15 June 2005.

European Commission, *Recommendations for Actions to Member States for Inclusion in their Lisbon Programmes*, COM(2005)24, companion document, 3 February 2005.

European Commission, Report "Better Lawmaking 2004", COM(2005)98, 21 March 2005 ("Simplification of the *acquis* remains a top priority, in particular for the Lisbon strategy").

European Commission, reports on the SLIM project, 2005 (available at *http://europa.eu.int/comm/internal_market/simplification/index_en.htm#slim*).

European Commission, Staff Working Paper, *The Economic Costs of Non-Lisbon*, SEC(2005)385, 15 March 2005.

European Commission, Staff Working Paper, Annex to the 2005 Communication on Better Regulation for Growth and Jobs in the European Union, *Minimising Administrative Costs Imposed by Legislation, Detailed Outline of a Possible EU Net Administrative Cost Model*, SEC(2005)175, 16 March 2005.

Commission, Communication on the Outcome of the screening of legislative proposals pending before the legislator, COM(2005)462, 27 September 2005.

European Commission, Communication on Implementing the Community Lisbon programme: A strategy for the simplification of the regulatory environment, COM(2005)535, 25 October 2005.

European Parliament, *Report on the Commission White Paper on European Governance*, A5-0399/2001, adopted by the European Parliament on 29 November 2001, OJ C 153E, 27 June 2002, pp. 314-322.

European Parliament, "Protocol on the application of the principles of subsidiarity and proportionality", OJ C310/207, 16 December 2004.

European Parliament, Resolution 2004/A5-0221, 24 March 2004.

High Level Group Chaired by Wim Kok, *Facing the Challenge*, 2004 (available at *http://europa.eu.int/growthandjobs/group/index_en.htm*).

Inter-Institutional Agreement on Better Lawmaking, OJ 2003/C 321/01, 23 December 2003.

Irish, Dutch, Luxembourg, UK, Austrian and Finnish Presidencies of the European Union, *Joint statement on Advancing Regulatory Reform in Europe*, 7 December 2004 (available at *http://www.hm-treasury.gov.uk/media/95A/52/6presidencies.pdf*).

Joint Statement (four presidencies) is available at *http://www.hm-treasury.gov.uk/media/47C54/jirf_0104.pdf*.

Mandelkern Group, Final Report, 2001 (available at *http://europa.eu.int/comm/secretariat_general/impact/docs/mandelkern.pdf*).

UK Presidency of the European Union, *Prospects for the EU in 2005 – The UK Presidency of the European Union*, presented to Parliament by the Secretary of State for Foreign and Commonwealth Affairs by Command of Her Majesty, June 2005.

UK Government Sources

Better Regulation Task Force (BRTF), *Good Policy Making: A guide to regulatory impact assessment*, London, Cabinet Office, 1999.

--------, *Alternatives to State Regulation*, 2000 (available at *http://www.brtf.gov.uk/docs/pdf/stateregulation.pdf*).

--------, *Principles of Good Regulation*, 2000 (available at *http://www.brtf.gov.uk/reports/principlesentry.asp*).

--------, Annual Report 2001/2002, *Champions of Better Regulation* (available at *http://www.brtf.gov.uk/docs/pdf/ar2002.pdf*).

--------, *Simplifying EU Law*, 2004 (available at *http://www.brtf.gov.uk/docs/pdf/simplebetter.pdf*).

--------, *Avoiding Regulatory Creep*, October 2004 (available at *http://www.brtf.gov.uk/docs/pdf/hiddenmenace.pdf*).

--------, *Make it Simple Make it Better – Simplifying EU Law*, 2004 (available at *http://www.brtf.gov.uk/docs/pdf/simplebetter.pdf*).

--------, *Get Connected – Effective Engagement in the EU*, September 2005 (available at *http://www.brtf.gov.uk/docs/pdf/getconnected.pdf*).

--------, *Regulation – Less is More. Reducing Burdens, Improving Outcomes*, 2005 (available at *http://www.brtf.gov.uk/docs/pdf/lessismore.pdf*).

Blair, T. and J. Cunningham, *Modernising Government*, 1999.

Cabinet Office, *Proposed Amendments to the Deregulation and Contracting Out Act 1994*, A Consultation Document, March 1999.

--------, *Regulatory Reform: the Government's Action Plan*, 10 December 2003 (available at *http://www.cabinetoffice.gov.uk/regulation/documents/regulatory_reform/pdf/rrap2003.pdf*).

--------, Press Release, "Cabinet Office kicks-off project to measure and cut red tape on business", CAB 043/05, 15 September 2005.

--------, *A Bill for Better Regulation: a Consultation Document*, 25 July 2005.

--------, Press Notice, *Transforming the Regulatory Landscape – Launch of a Consultation on a Bill for Better Regulation*, 2005 (available at *http://www.cabinetoffice.gov.uk/regulation/news/2005/050720_bill.asp*).

House of Commons, White Paper, *Lifting the Burden*, Cmnd 9751, 1985.

--------, White Paper, *Building Business – Not Barriers*, Cmnd 9794, 1986.

--------, Second Special Report of the Deregulation Committee, 2000 (available at *http://www.publications.parliament.uk/pa/cm199900/cmselect/cmdereg/488 48804.htm*).

--------, Research Paper No. 04/52, *Small Firms: Red Tape*, 28 June 2004.

National Audit Office (NAO), *Evaluation of Regulatory Impact Assessments Compendium Report 2004-05* (HC 341 Session 2004-2005).

––––––––, *Evaluation of Regulatory Impact Assessments Compendium Report 2003-04* (HC 358 Session 2003-04).

OFCOM, *Better Policy Making. Ofcom's Approach to Impact Assessment*, 2005 (available at *http://www.ofcom.org.uk/about/accoun/policy_making/guidelines.pdf*).

OFT, *Guidelines for Competition Assessment – A guide for policymakers completing regulatory impact assessments*, OFT355, 2002.

OFGEM, Guidance on Impact Assessment, 2005 (available at *http://www.ofgem.gov.uk/temp/ofgem/cache/cmsattach/11688_14805.pdf*).

RIU, *Better Policy Making: A Guide to Regulatory Impact Assessment* (available at *http://www.cabinet-office.gov.uk/regulation/docs/europe/pdf/tpguide.pdf*).

RIU, *Better Policy Making: Checklist to Ensure Good Quality European Legislation* (available at *http://www.cabinet-office.gov.uk/regulation/docs/europe/pdf/euchecklist.pdf*).

RIU, *Report on Improving UK Handling of European Legislation* (available at *http://www.cabinet-office.gov.uk/regulation/docs/europe/word/pqagssrep.doc*).

RIU, *Transposition Guide: How to Implement European Directives Effectively* (available at *http://www.cabinet-office.gov.uk/regulation/docs/europe/pdf/tpguide.pdf*).

UK Cabinet Office, *Opportunity for All in a World of Change*, White Paper On Enterprise, Skills And Innovation, 2001 (available at *http://www.dti.gov.uk/opportunityforall*).

UK Treasury, *Green Book: Appraisal and Evaluation in Central Government*, 2003 (available at *http://www.hm-treasury.gov.uk/media/05553/Green_Book_03.pdf*).

––––––––,*Chancellor Launches Better Regulation Action Plan*, Press Notice, 24 May 2005.

US Government Sources

Executive Order 11,821 of 27 November 1974 (available at *http://www.thecre.com/ombpapers/ExecutiveOrder11821.htm*).

Executive Order 11,949 of 31 December 1976 (available at *http://www.thecre.com/ombpapers/ExecutiveOrder11949.htm*).

Executive Order 12,291 of 17 February 1981 (available at *http://www.thecre.com/pdf/EO12291.PDF*).

GAO (General Accounting Office), *OMB's Role in the Reviews of Agencies' Draft Rules and the Transparency of these Reviews*, US Government, Washington, D.C., 2003.

OIRA (Office of Information and Regulatory Affairs), Circular D-4, 17 September 2003.

OMB (Office of Management and Budget) ('Quality of Life Review'), *Agency regulations, standards, and guidelines pertaining to environmental quality, consumer protection, and occupational and public health and safety*, 5 October 1971 (available at *http://www.thecre.com/ombpapers/QualityofLife1.htm*).

————, Draft *Report on the Costs and Benefits of Federal Regulations*, 2005 (available at *http://www.whitehouse.gov/omb/inforeg/regpol-reports_congress.html*).

OMB Watch and Public Citizen, *Voodoo Accounting: The Toll of President Bush's Regulatory Moratorium*, August 1992.

White House, Memorandum on the "Comprehensive Review of Federal Regulatory Programs", 15 December 1986.

————, Executive Order 12866, *Regulatory Planning and Review*, Federal Register 58, Washington, D.C.: The White House, 30 September 1993.

————, *Fact Sheet on Reagan's Initiatives to Reduce Regulatory Burdens*, 18 February 1981 (available at *http://www.thecre.com/pdf/Reagan_RegainInitiatives.pdf* – visited 2 August 2005).

APPENDIX A. LIST OF ExIAs ANALYSED

	Lead DG	Date	Title	ExIA	Proposal
71	COMP	07/06/2005	State Aid Action Plan - Less and better targeted state aid: a roadmap for state aid reform 2005-2009	SEC(2005)795	COM(2005)107
70	DEV	12/04/2005	Accelerating progress towards attaining the Millennium Development Goals - Financing for Development and Aid Effectiveness	SEC(2005)454	COM(2005)133
69	DEV	12/04/2005	Accelerating progress towards achieving the Millennium Development Goals - The European Union's contribution	SEC(2005)452	COM(2005)132
68	EAC	06/04/2005	Decision of the European Parliament and of the Council establishing for the period 2007-2013 the programme "Citizens for Europe" to promote active European citizenship	SEC(2005)442	COM(2005)116
67	EAC	30/05/2005	Communication on "Addressing the concerns of young people in Europe - implementing the European Youth Pact and promoting active citizenship"	SEC(2005)693	COM(2005)206
66	EMPL	09/02/2005	Communication on the Social Agenda	SEC(2005)177	COM(2005)33
65	EMPL	01/06/2005	Communication on Non-discrimination and equal opportunities for all - a framework strategy	SEC(2005)689	COM(2005)224
64	ENTR	06/04/2005	Decision of the European Parliament and of the Council establishing a Competitiveness and Innovation Framework Programme (2007-2013)	SEC(2005)433	COM(2005)121
63	ENV	2005/	Communication on Winning the Battle against Global Climate Change	SEC(2005)180	COM(2005)35
62	ENV	06/04/2005	Council Regulation establishing a Rapid Response and Preparedness Instrument for major emergencies	SEC(2005)439	COM(2005)113

61	FISH	06/04/2005	Council Regulation establishing Community financial measures for the implementation of the Common Fisheries Policy and in the area of the Law of the Sea	SEC(2005)426	COM(2005)117
60	INFSO	01/06/2005	Communication on "i2010 - a European Information Society for growth and employment"	SEC(2005)717	COM(2005)229
59	JLS	14/02/2005	Communication on a EU Drugs Action Plan (2005-2008)	SEC(2005)216	COM(2005)45
58	JLS	06/04/2005	General Programme on Fundamental Rights and Justice	SEC(2005)434	COM(2005)122
57	JLS	06/04/2005	General Programme Security and Safeguarding Liberties	SEC(2005)436	COM(2005)124
56	JLS	06/04/2005	General Programme Solidarity and Management of Migration Flows	SEC(2005)435	COM(2005)123
55	REGIO	06/04/2005	Regulation of the European Parliament and of the Council establishing the European Union Solidarity Fund	SEC(2005)447	COM(2005)108
54	RELEX	12/04/2005	Communication on the "Tenth Anniversary of the Euro-Mediterranean Partnership: A work programme to meet the challenges for the next five years	SEC(2005)483	COM(2005)139
53	RTD	06/04/2005	Decision of the European Parliament and of the Council concerning the seventh framework programme of the European Community for research, technological development and demonstration activities (2007-2013)	SEC(2005)430	COM(2005)119
52	SANCO	28/04/2005	Council Directive on Community measures for the control of Avian Influenza / Council Decision amending Council Decision 90/424/EEC on expenditure in the veterinary field	SEC(2005)549	COM(2005)171
51	SANCO	06/04/2005	Health and Consumer Protection Strategy and Programme	SEC(2005)425	COM(2005)115
50	TAXUD	06/04/2005	Communication on the Community programmes Customs 2013 and Fiscal 2013	SEC(2005)423	COM(2005)111
49	DEV	20/07/2004	Council Regulation establishing a voluntary FLEGT licensing scheme for imports of timber into the European Community	SEC(2004)977	COM(2004)515

48	EMPL	21/04/2004	Recast of the gender equality Directives	SEC(2004)482	COM(2004)279
47	EMPL	22/09/2004	Directive amending Directive 2003/88/EC concerning certain aspects of the organisation of working time	SEC(2004)1154	COM(2004)607
46	ENTR	29/09/2004	Regulation on medicinal products for paediatric use and amending Council Regulation (EEC) No 1786/92, Directive 2001/83/EC and Regulation (EC) No 726/2004	SEC(2004)1144	COM(2004)599
45	ENTR	25/10/2004	Directive laying down rules on nominal quantities for pre-packed products, repealing Council Directives 75/106/EEC and 80/232/EEC, and amending Council Directive 76/211/EEC	SEC(2004)1298	COM(2004)708
44	ENV	25/02/2004	Environment & Standardisation	SEC(2004)206	COM(2004)130
43	ENV	09/06/2004	Environment & Health Action Plan	SEC(2004)729	COM(2004)416(1) COM(2004)416(2)
42	ENV	23/07/2004	Directive establishing an infrastructure for spatial information in the Community (INSPIRE)	SEC(2004)980	COM(2004)516
41	FISH	28/04/2004	Council Regulation establishing a Community Fisheries Control Agency	SEC(2004)448	COM(2004)289
40	INFSO	17/05/2004	Update of eEurope 2005 Action Plan	SEC(2004)608	COM(2004)380
39	INFSO	30/07/2004	Communication on interoperability of digital interactive television services	SEC(2004)1028	COM(2004)541
38	JAI	12/02/2004	Council Decision establishing the European Refugee Fund for the period 2005 2010	SEC(2004)161	COM(2004)102
37	JAI	28/04/2004	Framework Decision on procedural rights in criminal proceedings	SEC(2004)491	COM(2004)328
36	JLS	28/12/2004	Regulation of the European Parliament and of the Council concerning the Visa Information System (VIS) and the exchange of data between Member States on short stay-visas	SEC(2004)1628	COM(2004)835
35	MARKT	21/04/2004	Directive on reinsurance	SEC(2004)443	COM(2004)273

34	MARKT	14/07/2004	Capital adequacy Directive	SEC(2004)921	COM(2004)486(1)
33	MARKT	14/09/2004	Directive amending Directive 98/71/EC on the legal protection of designs	SEC(2004)1097	COM(2004)582
32	MARKT	29/12/2004	Communication on an Action plan for the implementation of the legal framework for electronic public procurement	SEC(2004)1639	COM(2004)841
31	TREN	03/03/2004	Directive amending Council Directive 91/440/EEC on the development of the Community's railways	SEC(2004)236	COM(2004)139
30	AGRI	14/07/2004	Council Regulation on support for rural development by the European Agricultural Fund for Rural Development	SEC(2004)931	COM(2004)490
29	EAC	14/07/2004	Decision establishing the Culture 2007 Programme (2007-2013)	SEC(2004)954	COM(2004)469
28	EAC	14/07/2004	Decision concerning the implementation of the MEDIA 2007 Programme	SEC(2004)955	COM(2004)470
27	EAC	14/07/2004	Decision creating the "Youth in action" Programme (2007-2013)	SEC(2004)960	COM(2004)471
26	EAC	14/07/2004	Decision establishing an integrated action programme in the field of lifelong learning	SEC(2004)971	COM(2004)474
25	EMPL	2004/07/14	Regulation on the European Social Fund	SEC(2004)924	COM(2004)493
24	ENV	15/07/2004	Communication on financing Natura 2000	SEC(2004)770	COM(2004)431
23	FISH	14/07/2004	Council Regulation on European Fisheries Fund	SEC(2004)965	COM(2004)497
22	REGIO	14/07/2004	Council Regulation laying down general provisions on the European Regional Development Fund, the European Social Fund and the Cohesion Fund	SEC(2004)924	COM(2004)492
21	AGRI	23/09/2003	Review of the Sugar Regime	SEC(2003)1022	COM(2003)554
20	AGRI	23/09/2003	Review of the Tobacco Regime	SEC(2003)1023	COM(2003)554
19	ECFIN	15/10/2003	Communication of the Commission on the state of play and development of the Euro-Med Facility	SEC(2003)1110	COM(2003)587

18	EMPL	14/01/2003	Review of the European Employment Strategy	Communication	COM(2003)6
17	EMPL	05/11/2003	Directive on non-discrimination on the basis of sex (art. 13)	SEC(2003)1213	COM(2003)657
16	ENTR	21/11/2003	Basic orientations for the sustainability of European Tourism	SEC(2003)1295	COM(2003)716
15	ENV	23/07/2003	Legislation on the Kyoto flexible instruments Joint Implementation (JI) and Clean Development Mechanism (CDM)	SEC(2003)785	COM(2003)403
14	ENV	06/10/2003	Directive of the European Parliament and of the Council concerning groundwater protection	SEC(2003) 1086	COM(2003)550
13	ENV	29/10/2003	Framework Legislation on Chemical Substances (establishing REACH)	SEC(2003) 1171	COM(2003)644
12	ENV	24/11/2003	Directive on batteries and accumulators	SEC(2003)1343	COM(2003)723
11	FISH	23/12/2003	Proposal for a Council Regulation establishing measures for the recovery of the sole stocks in the Western Channel and the Bay of Biscay	SEC(2003)1480	COM(2003)819
10	FISH	23/12/2003	Proposal for a Council Regulation establishing measures for the recovery of the southern hake stock and the Norway lobster stocks in the Cantabrian Sea and Western Iberian peninsula	SEC(2003)1481	COM(2003)818
9	INFSO	15/09/2003	Communication on intelligent vehicles and road safety	SEC(2003)963	COM(2003)542
8	INFSO	17/09/2003	Communication on the transition from analogue broadcasting to digital broadcasting: Digital switchover in Europe	SEC(2003)992	COM(2003)541
7	JAI	03/06/2003	Communication on immigration, integration and employment	SEC(2003)694	COM(2003)336
6	MARKT	13/01/2004	Proposal for a directive on services in the internal market	SEC(2004)21	COM(2004)2
5	RELEX	28/10/2003	European Initiative for Democracy and Human Rights Regulations 975/1999 and 976/1999	SEC(2003)1170	COM(2003)639

4	SANCO	18/06/2003	Framework Directive of the European Parliament and of the Council on fair commercial practices	SEC(2003)724	COM(2003)356
3	TREN	01/10/2003	Decision replacing Decision 1692/96/EC on the Community guidelines for the development of the Tran-European Network in the field of transport (TEN guidelines)	SEC(2003)1060	COM(2003)564
2	TREN	10/12/2003	Directive on Security of Supply for Electricity	SEC(2003)1368	COM(2003)740
1	TREN	10/12/2003	Decision laying down guidelines for Trans-European energy networks	SEC(2003)1369	COM(2003)742

APPENDIX B. LIST OF SCORECARD ITEMS

Item Number	Variables
	Estimation of costs
1	Stated costs exist
2	Quantified at least some costs
3	Monetised at least some costs
4	Monetised all or nearly all costs
5	Provided best estimate of total cost
6	Provided range for total costs
7	Associate costs w/EU institutions
8	Associate costs/non-EU institution
9	Associate costs with producers (BIA)
10	Provided best estimate and range for total costs
	Estimation of benefits
11	Stated benefits exists
12	Quantified at least some benefits
13	Monetised at least some benefits
14	Monetised all or nearly all benefits
15	Provided best estimate of total benefits
16	Provided range for total benefits
17	Monetised safety benefits
18	Monetised health benefits
19	Monetised pollution reduction benefits (not health related)
20	Monetised pollution reduction benefits (health related)
21	Provide best estimate or range for total benefits
22	Provided best estimate and range for total benefits
23	Monetised any health-related benefit
	Comparison of costs and benefits
24	Calculated net benefits
25	Provided a best estimate of net benefits
26	Provided a range for net benefits
27	Calculated cost effectiveness
28	Provided a best estimate of cost effectiveness
29	Provided a range for cost effectiveness
30	Provided a point estimate or range for total cost effectiveness

31	Had positive net benefits
32	Calculated net benefits or cost effectiveness
33	Calculated net benefits and cost effectiveness
53	Calculated both point estimate and range for net benefits
54	Calculated either point estimate or range for net benefits
	Evaluation of alternatives
34	Gave at least one alternative standard level
35	Considered at least one alternative policy option
36	Quantified alternatives (costs)
37	Monetised alternatives (costs)
38	Quantified alternatives (benefits)
39	Monetised alternative (benefits)
40	Cost effectiveness of alternatives
41	Net benefits of alternatives
42	Calculated net benefits or cost effectiveness of alternatives
43	Considered some alternative
	Clarity of presentation
44	Contain executive summary
45	Summary contains tables
	Consistent use of analytical assumptions
46	Identified euro year
47	Used consistent euro year
48	Identified discount rate
49	Used consistent discount rate
50	Discount rate = 4%
51	Consistent costs and benefits
52	Identified and consistently used discount rate and euro year
	Lives
55	Point estimate for numbers of lives saved
56	Range estimates for number of lives saved
57	What was the point (or range) estimate of lives saved?
58	Point estimate for numbers of life-years saved
59	Range estimate for number of life-years saved
60	What was the point (or range) estimate of life-years saved?
	VSL
61	Point estimate for VSL
62	Range estimate for VSL
63	Point estimate for VSLY

64	Range estimate for VSLY
65	What was the point (and/or range) estimate of VSL or VSLY)
66	Did IIA give € year for VSL (or VSLY)?
67	What was the € year for VSL (or VSLY)?
	Discount rate
68	Point estimate for discount rate
69	Range estimate for discount rate
70	What was the point (and/or range) estimate of discount rate?
71	Did IIA specify real or nominal discount rate?
72	Was the discount rate real or nominal?
	Executive summary
73	ES presented at least some monetised costs
74	ES presented at least some monetised benefits
75	ES presented any measure of cost effectiveness
76	ES presented any estimate of net benefits
77	ES offer a best judgment of how benefits and costs compare
78	ES summarised any non-quantified benefits
79	ES summarised any non-quantified costs
	Other Items
80	Competitiveness proofing
81	Environmental impact assessed
82	Social impact assessed
83	Administrative burdens assessed
84	CBA, CEA, risk-risk analysis
85	Consultation reported
86	Consultation led to changes
87	Data from affected interests
88	Provision for review
89	Zero option considered
90	Consequence on single market
91	Considered the *acquis*
92	Considered soft law
93	Considered self-regulation
94	Considered co-regulation/open method of coordination
95	Considered subsidiarity
96	Considered proportionality
97	Sensitivity test
98	Use of external expertise

APPENDIX C. SCORECARD RESULTS

Item	Variables	2003	2004	2005
	Estimation of costs			
1	Stated costs exist	66.7%	74.1%	81.8%
2	Quantified at least some costs	42.9%	40.7%	36.4%
3	Monetised at least some costs	42.9%	40.7%	36.4%
4	Monetised all or nearly all costs	28.6%	33.3%	18.2%
5	Provided best estimate of total cost	19.0%	22.2%	13.6%
6	Provided range for total costs	14.3%	14.8%	9.1%
7	Associate costs w/EU institutions	9.5%	29.6%	27.3%
8	Associate costs/non-EU institution	9.5%	7.4%	0.0%
9	Associate costs with producers (BIA)	33.3%	11.1%	0.0%
10	Provided best estimate and range for total costs	4.8%	90.9%	4.5%
	Estimation of benefits			
11	Stated benefits exists	95.2%	100.0%	90.9%
12	Quantified at least some benefits	57.1%	33.3%	22.7%
13	Monetised at least some benefits	47.6%	22.2%	18.2%
14	Monetised all or nearly all benefits	23.8%	14.8%	4.5%
15	Provided best estimate of total benefits	19.0%	14.8%	4.5%
16	Provided range for total benefits	4.8%	3.7%	0.0%
17	Monetised safety benefits	14.3%	0.0%	0.0%
18	Monetised health benefits	4.8%	0.0%	4.5%
19	Monetised pollution reduction benefits (not health related)	14.3%	3.7%	0.0%
20	Monetised pollution reduction benefits (health related)	0.0%	0.0%	4.5%
21	Provide best estimate or range for total benefits	19.0%	18.5%	0.0%
22	Provided best estimate and range for total benefits	4.8%	0.0%	0.0%
23	Monetised any health-related benefit	4.8%	0.0%	9.1%
	Comparison of costs and benefits			
24	Calculated net benefits	28.6%	18.5%	4.5%
25	Provided a best estimate of net benefits	23.8%	14.8%	0.0%
26	Provided a range for net benefits	4.8%	3.7%	4.5%
27	Calculated cost effectiveness	0.0%	18.5%	4.5%

28	Provided a best estimate of cost effectiveness	0.0%	14.8%	4.5%
29	Provided a range for cost effectiveness	0.0%	3.7%	0.0%
30	Provided a point estimate or range for total cost effectiveness	0.0%	18.5%	4.5%
31	Had positive net benefits	33.3%	40.7%	4.5%
32	Calculated net benefits or cost effectiveness	28.6%	33.3%	9.1%
33	Calculated net benefits and cost effectiveness	0.0%	3.7%	0.0%
53	Calculated both point estimate and range for net benefits	0.0%	0.0%	0.0%
54	Calculated either point estimate or range for net benefits	28.6%	18.5%	4.5%

Evaluation of alternatives

34	Gave at least one alternative standard level	9.5%	0.0%	0.0%
35	Considered at least one alternative policy option	81.0%	92.6%	77.3%
36	Quantified alternatives (costs)	23.8%	22.2%	4.5%
37	Monetised alternatives (costs)	19.0%	22.2%	4.5%
38	Quantified alternatives (benefits)	33.3%	11.1%	0.0%
39	Monetised alternative (benefits)	19.0%	7.4%	0.0%
40	Cost effectiveness of alternatives	9.5%	14.8%	0.0%
41	Net benefits of alternatives	19.0%	11.1%	0.0%
42	Calculated net benefits or cost effectiveness of alternatives	28.6%	22.2%	0.0%
43	Considered some alternative	71.4%	81.5%	72.7%

Clarity of presentation

44	Contain executive summary	23.8%	3.7%	18.2%
45	Summary contains tables	4.8%	3.7%	9.1%

Consistent use of analytical assumptions

46	Identified euro year	4.8%	0.0%	0.0%
47	Used consistent euro year	4.8%	0.0%	0.0%
48	Identified discount rate	9.5%	0.0%	0.0%
49	Used consistent discount rate	4.8%	0.0%	0.0%
50	Discount rate = 4%	9.5%	0.0%	0.0%
51	Consistent costs and benefits	9.5%	3.7%	0.0%
52	Identified and consistently used discount rate and euro year	4.8%	0.0%	0.0%

Lives

55	Point estimate for numbers of lives saved	0.0%	0.0%	0.0%
56	Range estimates for number of lives saved	0.0%	0.0%	0.0%

57	What was the point (or range) estimate of lives saved?	0.0%	0.0%	0.0%
58	Point estimate for numbers of life-years saved	4.8%	0.0%	0.0%
59	Range estimate for number of life-years saved	0.0%	0.0%	0.0%
60	What was the point (or range) estimate of life-years saved?	0.0%	0.0%	0.0%
VSL				
61	Point estimate for VSL	0.0%	0.0%	0.0%
62	Range estimate for VSL	0.0%	0.0%	0.0%
63	Point estimate for VSLY	0.0%	0.0%	0.0%
64	Range estimate for VSLY	4.8%	0.0%	0.0%
65	What was the point (and/or range) estimate of VSL or VSLY)	4.8%	3.7%	4.5%
66	Did IIA give € year for VSL (or VSLY)?	4.8%	0.0%	0.0%
67	What was the € year for VSL (or VSLY)?	4.8%	3.7%	4.5%
Discount rate				
68	Point estimate for discount rate	9.5%	0.0%	0.0%
69	Range estimate for discount rate	0.0%	0.0%	0.0%
70	What was the point (and/or range) estimate of discount rate?	9.5%	7.4%	9.1%
71	Did IIA specify real or nominal discount rate?	0.0%	0.0%	0.0%
72	Was the discount rate real or nominal?	0.0%	0.0%	0.0%
Executive Summary (ES)				
73	ES presented at least some monetised costs	0.0%	3.7%	0.0%
74	ES presented at least some monetised benefits	0.0%	3.7%	4.5%
75	ES presented any measure of cost effectiveness	0.0%	0.0%	0.0%
76	ES presented any estimate of net benefits	0.0%	0.0%	4.5%
77	ES offer a best judgment of how benefits and costs compare	0.0%	3.7%	0.0%
78	ES summarised any non-quantified benefits	23.8%	3.7%	9.1%
79	ES summarised any non-quantified costs	0.0%	3.7%	0.0%
Other Items				
80	Competitiveness-proofing	23.8%	18.5%	22.7%
81	Environmental impact assessed	81.0%	59.3%	54.5%
82	Social impact assessed	81.0%	81.5%	81.8%
83	Administrative burdens assessed	19.0%	37.0%	13.6%
84	CBA, CEA, risk-risk analysis	38.1%	22.2%	4.5%
85	Consultation reported	100.0%	100.0%	81.8%
86	Consultation led to changes	52.4%	55.6%	45.5%

87	Data from affected interests	0.0%	33.3%	18.2%
88	Provision for review	28.6%	70.4%	68.2%
89	Zero option considered	85.7%	81.5%	81.8%
90	Consequence on single market	47.6%	40.7%	31.8%
91	Considered the *acquis*	33.3%	37.0%	13.6%
92	Considered soft law	14.3%	3.7%	18.2%
93	Considered self-regulation	4.8%	11.1%	4.5%
94	Considered co-regulation/open method of coordination	4.8%	7.4%	13.6%
95	Considered subsidiarity	71.4%	70.4%	45.5%
96	Considered proportionality	71.4%	63.0%	36.4%
97	Sensitivity test	14.3%	3.7%	0.0%

Appendix D.
Summary of Recommendations

Roadmap 1 - Methodology

1.1 Increase use of quantitative analysis.

1.2 Increase quali-quantitative comparison of available alternatives.

1.3 Enable assessment of regulatory creep and compliance costs.

1.4 Create an independent oversight agency as consultant, supervisor and regulatory clearinghouse.

1.5 Increase the use and consistency of discount rates.

1.6 Mandate inclusion of soft law, self- and co-regulation in the alternatives.

1.7 Introduce sanctions for insufficient or unsatisfactory IA.

1.8 Increase reliance on external expertise.

Roadmap 2 - Proportionality

2.1 Indicate proposals that require quantitative CBA of all alternatives.

2.2 Indicate proposals that require qualitative assessment of alternatives, and quantitative CBA of the selected option.

2.3 Indicate clearly when lead DGs can resort to cost-effectiveness, risk-risk or compliance cost analysis instead of CBA.

2.4 Appoint an external oversight agency in charge of supervising the application of the proportionality principle by lead DGs.

2.5 State that whenever ExIAs will not carry a justified application of the Treaty-based proportionality principle, they will be rejected as incomplete.

2.6 In case of co-decision procedures, the Parliament and the Council will not accept the proposal until it accounts for Treaty-based proportionality.

2.7 An external oversight agency should supervise the application of the methodological proportionality principle by lead DGs.

Roadmap 3 – Sector-specific impact assessment

3.1 Define the modules of the IIA model that should be adapted to the sector.

3.2 Enable each DG to propose its own methodology.

3.3 Involve the ERG for assessments that will be carried out by NRAs.

3.4 Provide for supervision, consultancy and clearance by an external audit.

3.5 Open defined procedures to public consultations for at least 60 days.

3.6 Provide for review of the defined methodology every three years.

3.7 Enable benchmarking of methodologies and lesson-drawing between DGs.

ROADMAP 4 – INTERNAL CONSISTENCY

4.1 Introduce sanction mechanisms.

4.2 Appoint a single ad hoc agency for the supervision of initiatives.

4.3 The agency will also supervise methodological consistency.

4.4 The agency will be in charge of reporting on overall impact of regulations.

ROADMAP 5 – CLARITY OF PRESENTATION

5.1 Always perform comparison between costs and benefits.

5.2 Improve clarity in the drafting.

5.3 Use comprehensive executive summaries.

5.4 Follow the standard IIA form.

5.5 Include the results obtained through external studies in the ExIa document.

ROADMAP 6 – PROMOTING CULTURAL CHANGE

6.1 Coordinate training initiatives.

6.2 Involve DGs in the development of methodologies.

6.3 Introduce control mechanisms for insufficient assessments.

ROADMAP 7 – *EX POST* MONITORING AND EVALUATION

7.1 Introduce methods of compliance testing.

7.2 Investigate reasons for non-compliance.

7.3 Enable performance testing.

7.4 Follow the recommendations of the IRQ Pilot Project.

7.5 Identify and publish best and worst practices.

7.6 Appoint independent body to monitor administrative burdens.

7.7 Schedule periodical testing.

7.8   Use external expertise for *una tantum* survey-based tests of cultural change.

Roadmap 8 – Subsidiarity

8.1   Improve transposition.

8.2   Issue a communication on RIA in member states.

8.3   Provide for gradual convergence on key issues.

8.4   Create a network of national RIA authorities to be coordinated by a new independent oversight agency at EU level.

Roadmap 9 – Competitiveness-proofing

9.1   Include competitiveness in the IIA standard model by issuing guidelines on how to perform competitiveness-proofing or competition assessment.

9.2   Involve CC at the interim stage between the preliminary IA and the ExIA.

9.3   Allow the CC to signal ExIA that do not sufficiently address competitiveness.

9.4   Involve DG COMP in the consultation process.

9.5   Introduce a competition filter test supported by the DG COMP.

Roadmap 10 – Creating a regulatory watchdog

10.1 Create a centralised regulatory unit rooted in the Commission's Secretariat-General.

10.2 Empower it with roles of advocacy, consulting, guidance, challenge, coordination of existing initiatives, training, yearly reporting and keeping institutional relations.

10.3 Allow for initial reliance on external expertise, and gradual development of in-house knowledge and competences.

RECENT CEPS PUBLICATIONS

CEPS Paperbacks (€25 in print or €20 in PDF)

Multilateralism or Regionalism? Trade Policy Options for the European Union, Guido Glania and Jürgen Matthes, December 2005

Europe's Hidden Capital Markets: Evolution, Architecture and Regulation of the European Bond Market, Jean-Pierre Casey and Karel Lannoo, November 2005

Democratisation in the European Neighbourhood, Michael Emerson (ed.), October 2005

Readings in European Security, Vol. 3, Dana H. Allin and Michael Emerson (eds), October 2005

Migration, Borders & Asylum: Trends and Vulnerabilities in EU Policy, Thierry Balzacq and Sergio Carrera, July 2005

Deep Integration: How Transatlantic Markets are Leading Globalization; Daniel S. Hamilton and Joseph P. Quinlan (eds), published jointly with the Center for Transatlantic Relations of Johns Hopkins University, June 2005

EMU at Risk, Daniel Gros, Thomas Mayer and Angel Ubide, 7th Annual Report of the CEPS Macroeconomic Policy Group, June 2005

CEPS Task Force Reports (€25 in print or €20 in PDF)

Achieving a Common Consolidated Corporate Tax Base in the EU, Malcolm Gammie, Silvia Giannini, Alexander Klemm, Andreas Oestreicher, Paola Parascandolo and Christoph Spengel, December 2005

Reviewing the EU Emissions Trading Scheme: Priorities for Short-Term Implementation of the Second Round of Allocation (Part I), Christian Egenhofer and Noriko Fujiwara, December 2005

Market Stimulation of Renewable Electricity in the EU: What Degree of Harmonisation to Support Mechanisms is Required?, Jaap Jansen, Kyriakos Gialoglou and Christian Egenhofer, October 2005

Towards a Global Climate Regime: Priority Areas for a Coherent EU Strategy, Christian Egenhofer and Louise van Schaik, May 2005

EU Financial Regulation and Supervision beyond 2005, Karel Lannoo and Jean-Pierre Casey, February 2005

Business Consequences of the EU Emissions Trading Scheme, Christian Egenhofer, Noriko Fujiwara and Kyriakos Gialoglou, February 2005

CEPS Research Reports in Finance and Banking (€40 in print/€30 in PDF)

The New Basel Capital Accord and SME Financing: SMEs and the New Rating Culture, Rym Ayadi, November 2005

CEPS Working Documents (€12 in print or free downloading)

Economic Regimes for Export: Extending the EU's Norms of Economic Governance into the Neighbourhood, Gergana Noutcheva and Michael Emerson, December 2005

The EU Budget Process and International Trade Liberalisation, David Kernohan, Jorge Núñez Ferrer and Andreas Schneider, October 2005

No Constitutional Treaty? Implications for the Area of Freedom, Security and Justice, Elspeth Guild and Sergio Carrera, September 2005

European Neighbourhood Policy: Enhancing Prospects for Reform in the Mashreq Countries, Stephen Jones and Michael Emerson, September 2005

The EU as an 'Intergovernmental' Actor in Foreign Affairs: Case Studies on the International Criminal Court and the Kyoto Protocol, Martijn L.P. Groenleer, and Louise G. van Schaik, August 2005

Integrated Border Management at the EU Level, Peter Hobbing, August 2005

Security, Integration and the Case for Regionalism in the EU Neighbourhood, Fabrizio Tassinari, July 2005

Russia-EU Relations: The Present Situation and Prospects, Sergei Karaganov, July 2005

Prospects for the Lisbon Strategy: How to Increase the Competitiveness of the European Economy?, Daniel Gros, July 2005

The Reluctant Debutante: The European Union as Promoter of Democracy in its Neighbourhood, Michael Emerson, Senem Aydın, Gergana Noutcheva, Nathalie Tocci, Marius Vahl and Richard Youngs, July 2005

Trade Adjustments following the Removal of Textile and Clothing Quotas, Christian Buelens, May 2005

Conflict Resolution in the Neighbourhood: Comparing the Role of the EU in the Turkish-Kurdish and Israeli-Palestinian Conflicts, Nathalie Tocci, March 2005

From Barcelona Process to Neighbourhood Policy: Assessments and Open Issues, Michael Emerson and Gergana Noutcheva, March 2005

'Integration' as a Process of Inclusion for Migrants? The Case of Long-Term Residents in the EU, Sergio Carrera, March 2005

Models for the European Neighbourhood Policy: The European Economic Area and the Northern Dimension, Marius Vahl, February 2005

The Widening Gap between Rhetoric and Reality in EU Policy towards the Israeli-Palestinian Conflict, Nathalie Tocci, January 2005